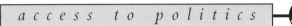

access to politics

LAW, ORDER
and the
JUDICIARY

access to politics

LAW, ORDER
and the
JUDICIARY

Peter Joyce

Series Editor: David Simpson

Hodder & Stoughton

A MEMBER OF THE HODDER HEADLINE GROUP

DEDICATION

To my wife Julie, and my daughters, Emmeline and Eleanor

ACKNOWLEDGEMENTS

The publishers would like to thank the following for permission to reproduce photographs:

PA News: pages 26, 42, 75 and 119; Yorkshire Post Newspapers Ltd: page 29.

Orders: please contact Bookpoint Ltd, 39 Milton Park, Abingdon, Oxon OX14 4TD. Telephone: (44) 01235 400414, Fax: (44) 01235 400454. Lines are open from 9.00–6.00, Monday to Saturday, with a 24 hour message answering service. Email address: orders@bookpoint.co.uk

British Library Cataloguing in Publication Data
A catalogue record for this title is available from The British Library

ISBN 0 340 757728

First published 1999, Peter Joyce
Impression number 10   9   8   7   6   5   4   3   2   1
Year   2005   2004   2003   2002   2001   2000   1999

Cover photo from PA News

Typeset by Transet Limited, Coventry, England.
Printed in Great Britain for Hodder & Stoughton Educational, a division of Hodder Headline plc, 338 Euston Road, London NW1 3BH by Redwood Books, Trowbridge, Wilts.

CONTENTS

PREFACE

A/AS Level syllabuses in Government and Politics aim to develop knowledge and understanding of the political system of the UK. They cover its local, national and European Union dimensions, and include comparative studies of aspects of other political systems, in order to ensure an understanding of the distinctive nature of the British political system. The minimum requirements for comparative study are aspects of systems with a separation of powers, how other systems protect the rights of individuals and how other electoral systems work.

Access to Politics is a series of concise topic books which cover the syllabus requirements, providing students with the necessary resources to complete the course successfully.

General advice on approaching exam questions

To achieve high grades you need to demonstrate consistency. Clearly address all parts of a question, make good use of essay plans or notes, and plan your time to cover all the questions.

Make your answers stand out from the crowd by using contemporary material to illustrate them. You should read a quality newspaper and listen to or watch appropriate programmes on radio and television.

Skills Advice

You should comprehend, synthesise and interpret political information in a variety of forms:

- Analyse and evaluate political institutions, processes and behaviour, political arguments and explanations.
- Identify parallels, connections, similarities and differences between aspects of the political systems studied.
- Select and organise relevant material to construct arguments and explanations leading to reasoned conclusions.
- Communicate the arguments with relevance, clarity and coherence, using vocabulary appropriate to the study of Government and Politics.

David Simpson

1

INTRODUCTION

THIS BOOK IS concerned with two broad areas – crime and disorder, and the judicial system. It primarily deals with the period since 1979, although it is sometimes necessary (as with the discussion of police governance) to discuss matters which occurred before this date. Chapter 2 discusses the importance of crime as a political issue and evaluates the responses to it by governments since 1979. Attention is devoted to the similarities and differences in the approach adopted by both major parties, and the chapter provides a detailed evaluation of the 1998 Crime and Disorder Act which will shape the state's reponse to crime (and especially juvenile crime) into the twenty-first century. Chapter 3 examines disorder which is discussed within the context of extra-parliamentary political activity. Demonstrations, industrial disputes, counter-cultural protest, and urban disorder have been selected for study. Explanations for the growth of extra-parliamentary politics since 1979 are evaluated, and the response of the State (in the form of public order legislation and measures to regulate the ability of unions to organise strikes) is analysed.

Chapters 4 and 5 focus on the judicial system. Chapter 4 discusses the composition of the legal profession, the organisation of the civil and criminal courts, the ability of judges to make law, and the system of trial by jury; an important aspect of the judicial system in many liberal democratic countries. Chapter 5 examines the constitutional position of the judiciary. Particular attention is devoted to the independence of the judiciary, focusing on key issues such as the appointments process for judges, the system of judicial review and the manner in which the 1992–1997 Conservative government sought to enhance its control over the activities of the judiciary.

Chapter 6 discusses the governance (ie, the control and accountability) of the police service. It analyses the tripartite system of police governance introduced by the 1964 Police Act, and the pressures for changes to the system of control and accountability which resulted in the 1984 Police and Criminal Evidence Act and the 1994 Police and Magistrates' Courts Act. This chapter also considers issues concerned with the structure and organisation of policing, analysing those pressures which have resulted in changes to the decentralised nature of policing.

The theme of the final chapter is civil liberties. Particular attention is devoted to the issue of racial violence. The response of the State (and especially the police service) is evaluated in detail, placing considerable attention on the contents and implementation of the 1999 report by Sir William Macpherson into the Metropolitan Police's failures in connection with the investigation of the murder of Stephen Lawrence in 1993.

Each chapter also contains revision hints and sample questions. The former are especially important as they seek to emphasise the way in which the material contained in the seven chapters is inter-related. A particular purpose of the revision hints, therefore, is to give guidance concerning how to plan an answer to a question which is based upon material from more than one chapter.

2

CRIME AND POLITICS

Introduction

CRIME IS A key political issue. The promise (or attainment) of success in combating crime may bring considerable political benefits. In the UK, for example, the promise to adopt a harsh approach to crime and disorder was a major factor in Margaret Thatcher's victory at the 1979 general election. Alternatively, deficiencies in the response by a government to these issues will be exploited by opposition parties, and will cost it public support. For example, the damaging effects which failures connected with crime and the criminal justice system may bring to a government, has been evidenced in Belgium: in October 1996, 300,000 people marched in protest through Brussels over police failures in connection with large scale kidnapping and murder of children carried out by Marc Dutroux. In 1998, Dutroux's escape from custody resulted in a parliamentary censure motion. The government narrowly won this, but only after ministers secured the resignation of the country's chief of police. Police and judicial failings in this case were a major issue in the 1999 Belgium general election.

Key Points

This chapter will discuss the following key issues:

- the extent and nature of crime since 1979, and issues related to its measurement
- the policies put forward by the Conservative party between 1979 and 1997 to remedy crime
- the approach to crime adopted by the Labour government after 1997, analysing the similarities with, and differences to, the solutions put forward by the Conservative party.

The Cost of the Criminal Justice System

The criminal justice system is a major element of public spending. It is necessary, therefore, to ensure that money is spent efficiently so that the public gets good value for its money. This concern influenced attempts by Conservative governments in the 1980s to impose controls on agencies within the criminal justice system. As the following figures illustrate, the cost of law and order in considerable. The figures for 1995/6 for England and Wales were as follows:

Police Service	£6,633 million
The CPS	£ 297 million
Magistrates Courts	£ 416 million
Lord Chancellor's Department	£ 744 million
Probation Service	£ 481 million
Prison Service	£1,658 million
Legal Aid	£1,443 million
Criminal Injuries Compensation	£ 251 million

Figures taken from Her Majesty's Inspectorate of Policing, *What Price Policing? A Study of Efficiency and Value for Money in the Police Service* (1998).

CRIME SINCE 1979

The extent of crime has been increasing in almost all Western industrialised societies, and official statistics indicate that it has been rising in England and Wales since 1955. When the Conservative government was elected to office in 1979, the number of recorded offences in England and Wales comprised around 2.5 million. When they left office in 1997, this figure had exceeded 5 million. Although, as will be argued later in this chapter, such official statistics do not provide a totally accurate picture concerning the level of crime within society, they do suggest that crime is a major problem.

An additional problem is the fear of crime. This affects large numbers of the population: 20 per cent of adults questioned in the 1996 British Crime Survey indicated they were very worried about the possibility of being burgled, mugged or having their cars stolen or broken into. Thus the actuality and fear of crime have an adverse effect on the quality of life for large numbers of people. In particular this human cost of crime affects women and elderly people who are frequently victims, and exerts a destructive impact on communities.

A disproportionate amount of crime is committed by young people, mainly young males. In 1994, according to figures published by the Audit Commission, two out of every five known offenders were below the age of 21, and a quarter were under 18. Most crime committed by young people aged between 14 and 17 was property-related, and the great bulk of this was committed by a small group of prolific, hardened offenders.

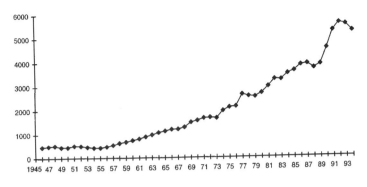

RECORDED CRIME IN ENGLAND AND WALES 1946–94

Source: Criminal Statistics, England and Wales (various issues).

THE MEASUREMENT OF CRIME

The success or failure of a government's crime policies is gauged by statistics. These form the basis on which members of the public judge the record of the government regarding crime. The main source of this evidence comes from official crime statistics.

OFFICIAL CRIME STATISTICS

Official crime statistics consist of figures collected by individual police forces which are forwarded to the Home Office. This enables information concerning the national trend to be provided. However, official crime statistics do not record all crimes which have been committed. A number of stages are involved in their construction whereby crimes which occur, fail to be recorded. These include:

- *awareness that a crime has been committed*: some crimes such as tax evasion have no obvious victim; other crimes such as theft may be attributed by the victim to carelessness, rather than due to another person's criminal actions.
- *deciding to report the crime to the police*: victims of crime may not always be willing to report it to the police. Victims of sexual or racial crimes may be reluctant to report them, due to a lack of confidence in the criminal justice system to respond to the complaints fairly.
- *recording of the incident by the police*: not all crimes reported to the police are subsequently recorded by them. Guidance is given by the Home Office concerning this matter which requests information only on 'notifiable offences'.

There are two important consequences of the above factors:

- *Official crime statistics tend to underplay the level of crime in society*: the gap between the volume of crime which is actually committed, and that which enters into official crime statistics, is referred to the **dark figure** of crime.
- *Official crime statistics give false impressions of rises or falls in the actual extent of crime*: for example, when official statistics suggest a rise in the level of crime, this may be due to the increased reporting of it, rather than a genuine increase in the level of such activity.

Clear up rates

Official figures also state the extent to which recorded crimes subsequently result in the apprehension of an offender. This **clear up** (or detection) rate is a major means for assessing the efficiency of the police service. However, as with the level of crime, statistics indicating clear up rates also provide a distorted picture of the real position.

One problem arises when a person convicted of an offence asks for similar crimes to be taken into consideration. This has the effect of recording them as cleared up, even though there is not necessarily any evidence to associate this person with them. Those who ask for offences to be taken into consideration do so in the hope this will secure a lighter sentence. In 1999 the Channel 4 programme, *Dispatches*, alleged that this process was subject to abuse – in one police force which they investigated (Nottinghamshire) officers induced criminals to confess to crimes regardless of whether or not they had committed them. This action enabled the crimes to be listed as detected, so that the force could present itself as efficient.

ALTERNATIVE METHODS TO STUDY THE EXTENT OF CRIMINAL ACTIVITY

The weaknesses discussed above concerning official crime statistics, have justified the use of other methods to gather more accurate information concerning the level of crime in society. These include self report studies and victimisation surveys.

Victimisation surveys

Victimisation surveys have been used in official studies such as the British Crime Survey since 1982. This involves interviewing a representative sample of members of the general public (around 15,000 in total) to extract information relating to their experience of crime during the previous year. This procedure makes it possible to contrast comparable categories of crime used by both the police and the British Crime Survey, and in particular to obtain information on crimes which are either not reported to the police or recorded by them. The 1998 British Crime Survey suggested that 16.4 million crimes had been committed in

1997, compared to the official statistics which stated that in the 12 months which ended in March 1998, 4.5 million crimes had been recorded.

A number of factors can affect the reliability of victimisation studies: eg, a respondent reporting an incident which occurred outside the period which is being surveyed; or a failure to remember minor incidents which took place during that time.

EXPLANATIONS FOR CRIME AFTER 1979

There are numerous reasons which may explain crime in any period of history. Broadly, however, a distinction can be drawn between explanations which attribute blame on the individual, and those which locate the explanation of crime in the operations of society.

Crime as the fault of the individual

There are many reasons to explain why the individual may be held responsible for crime. These include moral failings (whereby an individual does not know right from wrong), and biological factors which in the twentieth century led scientists on a search for the 'criminal gene' – to establish whether a person's biological make-up may be responsible for them committing crime. Additionally, the state of a person's mental health may result in criminal actions.

Crime as the fault of society

A further broad range of explanations suggest that crime may arise as the result of society failing individuals or groups of people. Factors such as unemployment, inadequate housing and poor recreational facilities may result in people turning to crime, either because this provides the only way in which they can provide for the necessaries of life, or because crime provides them excitement to relieve monotomy associated with a life of social deprivation. Crime may also provide people in this situation with a way of securing some form of self esteem (if only from their peers), which mainstream society denies to them because of their social disadvantage.

Marxist views of crime

The view that the operations of society cause crime is prominent in Marxist thinking. Marxists view the economic system, and the unequal property relations which this generates, as the root cause of crime. They assert that crime is based upon material inequality, and that the only viable solution to this situation is to abolish the capitalist system, since its unavoidably exploitive nature limits the potential of meaningful social reform. This view has, however, been criticised for two reasons:

- It fails to encompass crime which may not be underlaid by economic motives, such as violence and sexual assault.

- It can glamorise criminal actions by depicting them as political statements directed against capitalism and its underlying values, in particular the work ethic and the sanctity of private property ownership.

Additionally, the approach adopted by Marxists tends to give the criminal the characteristics of Robin Hood, who robbed the rich to give to the poor. In reality, however, much crime is not of this nature but is directed against members of the working class.

THE CONSERVATIVE PARTY'S RESPONSE TO CRIME

Support of the existing social order is a key concern of conservativism, and underpins the attitude of this party towards crime, disorder and moral misbehaviour. Conservatives assert that those who commit crime are responsible for their actions; they are making a rational choice, and their action is based on moral failing such as greed. They reject deficiencies in the operations of society being responsible for crime. In 1993 the then Home Secretary, Michael Howard, stated that he would have 'no truck with trendy theories that try to explain crime away by blaming socio-economic factors'. He emphasised that 'criminals are responsible for crime, and they should be held to account for their actions'. He insisted that 'trying to pass the buck is wrong, counterproductive and dangerous'.

POLICIES PURSUED BY CONSERVATIVE GOVERNMENTS, 1979-1997

The main features of the approach adopted by Conservative governments, which placed the needs of society ahead of the desire to reform criminals, are discussed below.

The regulation of social behaviour by legislative sanction

The attempt to regulate social behaviour by legislative sanction formed a major aspect of Conservative policy after 1979. The desire to deter anti-social behaviour (especially that identified with young people) was contained in a range of measures which culminated in the 1994 Criminal Justice and Public Order Act. This sought to combat actions such as football hooliganism, disorderly conduct, under-age drinking, 'acid house' parties and raves, through the provision of wider police powers or stiffer penalties for those who engaged in such pursuits.

Retribution

Although a 'tough' response to crime is designed to deter such actions, the main intention of retribution is to ensure that criminals are punished for their actions. A significant feature of this punative approach towards law and order after 1979 was to 'get tough' with criminals who would receive the 'just deserts' for their crimes. Initially an attempt was made to distinguish between non-violent offences (which could be responded to with a range of community-based, non-custodial, punishments) and violent crimes which required a term of imprisonment. This twin track approach underpinned the 1991 Criminal Justice Act.

However, the perception that the general public viewed sentences other than custodial ones as a 'soft option' prompted the government to re-think its approach towards crime. At the 1993 Conservative Party Conference, Michael Howard put forward a 'back to basics' approach to law and order, emphasising the importance of imprisonment as a key aspect of the government's response to crime. A particular target was the cautioning rather than prosecution of offenders. He asserted that 'nothing infuriates people more than to hear of offenders receiving cautions again and again, rather than being brought to trial'. This resulted in the publication of new guidance to the police on cautioning on 29 October 1993. Many of these proposals were subsequently contained in the 1994 Police and Magistrates' Courts Act and the 1994 Criminal Justice and Public Order Act.

Two years later, tougher sentences were presented as a key aspect of the government's anti-crime strategy. It was summarised in Michael Howard's statement, 'if you don't want the time, don't do the crime'. This 'prison works' philosophy resulted in the size of Britain's prison population soaring from around 45,000 in 1981, to over 60,000 by 1997. The perception that the judiciary was too lenient on criminals resulted in the introduction of mandatory sentences in the 1997 Crime (Sentences) Act (which is discussed in chapter 5). It was estimated that this measure would place an additional 10,800 'career criminals' behind bars.

JUVENILE CRIME – THE RETRIBUTIVE APPROACH

The retributive approach was also adopted towards juvenile crime. Conservatives wanted to convince the public that persistent or serious juvenile offenders were being appropriately punished for their action.

The harsh response was initially put forward in the 1982 Criminal Justice Act. Short sentences would be served in detention centres in which a disciplined regime was in operation, popularly referred to as the 'short, sharp shock'. The Act also provided for the possibility of harsher sentences for youth crime, and restricted the discretionary powers of social workers, seeking to ensure that decisions of Youth Courts were based on the hard facts concerning crimes, rather than a subjective assessment of a child's welfare needs.

Subsequently, the image of persistent juvenile offenders was presented as a political reason for introducing a more coercive approach towards youth crime; this resulted in the increased use of custodial sentences. In 1993 the then Home Secretary, Kenneth Clarke, promised to introduce measures to tackle 'nasty, persistent little offenders'. These were introduced in the 1994 Criminal Justice and Public Order Act.

The punitive response to juvenile crime was subject to a range of criticisms. In addition to the costs of custodial regimes for young offenders, it was argued that institutions which aimed to knock the criminal spirit out of young offenders, raised the possibility of brutalising juveniles who were thus likely to reoffend, perhaps in a more violent manner.

The remoralisation of society

Conservatives placed strong emphasis on the importance of restoring traditional moral values in order to prevent crime. They looked beyond the criminal justice system to encourage people to make the correct moral choices, and emphasised the importance of institutions such as schools and the family to instill into children the ability to discern right from wrong. This aspect of their approach was especially influenced by the American writer, Charles Murray, who contended that illegitimacy was the key social evil. This problem, he believed, needed to be eradicated by measures which included abolishing welfare payments to single mothers.

In the early 1980s Margaret Thatcher chaired a Cabinet Committee on family policy. Little emerged from this initiative, but in 1993 the Conservative Party's 'Back to Basics' campaign scapegoated single mothers for the level of crime and delinquency in society. At the 1993 Conservative Party Conference, the then Education Secretary, John Patten, stated that 'the family has always been fundamental to education because it is in the family that children learn the difference between right and wrong. It is the family that instils moral values and it is the family that gives a child a sense of purpose and belonging'. In 1996 a moral code for schools was proposed by the National Forum for Values in Education. This listed the values which should be incorporated into teaching, and was designed to counter the 'no blame, no shame society'. The Education Secretary, Gillian Shepherd, wanted it to be strengthened to provide a clear indication of family values, including marriage.

No compassion towards criminals

A further aspect of the Conservative Party's approach towards crime and disorder was an aggressive form of denunciation of criminal actions. This was designed to build consent for coercive responses to the crime and disorder, especially when associated with the socially deprived living in inner city areas. The use of language and imagery which (as with racism) sought to deny humanity to those people whose actions threaten social harmony, constituted an important aspect of Conservative policy to secure legitimacy for punitive action against those who transgressed key social values. Car thieves, for example, were depicted as 'hyenas' in campaigns mounted by the Home Office. The main danger with such an approach is that those depicted as animals may respond accordingly, resulting in a more violent and less safe society.

The resurrection of the work ethic

The Conservative Party viewed work not as a social right but as an important form of social discipline which would curtail crime. The main initiative to achieve this was contained in the 1995 Jobseekers Act. This legislation replaced unemployment benefit and income support, by a jobseeker's allowance for unemployed people from April 1996. This legislation also altered benefit rules: benefit would be stopped where the behaviour of an unemployed person actively prevented him/her from finding work. The Act additionally created a workfare programme – claimants would be required to undertake tasks of benefit to the community, where such work would improve the claimant's job prospects.

THE CONSEQUENCE OF CONSERVATIVE POLICIES:
SOCIAL EXCLUSION

One aspect of government policy after 1979 was to isolate geographically the underclass in inner-city locations from which there was little or no hope of escape. The *Observer* on 3 November 1996 argued that opportunities for mobility by children of disadvantaged parents was receding: 'the steady march of [school] league tables, hotch-potch selection and opting out, create an educational system in which there are sink schools at the bottom'. The perception that school league tables were a mechanism of social isolation was later emphasised by the *Independent on Sunday* on 8 December 1996, which observed that parents who wished to get their children into comprehensive schools which fared well in the league tables, were willing to pay above the market price for property in order to move into the catchment area for such schools. This denies access to the best education for people who cannot afford to live in that area.

THE LABOUR PARTY'S RESPONSE TO CRIME

The Labour Party had traditionally differed from the approach to crime endorsed by Conservatives. They believed it was necessary to tackle the problem at its roots, rather than focusing on the need for harsh actions against those who broke the law. While in opposition, Labour asserted the importance of social conditions such as unemployment, inner-city decay and the widening gap between the most and least prosperous members of society, as conditions which bred crime. Such policies, underlaid by the Conservative Party's emphasis on individualism, could be held responsible for creating crime and disorder. However, Labour's traditional attitude towards this subject was affected by the fact that the Conservative Party's attitude to crime was popular. This led to many of the ideas associated with the Conservative Party being endorsed by 'New' Labour in the 1990s, thus enabling this party to enter the 1997 general election firmly identified by the public as the party of law and order. Labour now emphasised their support for:

- *the family*: the Conservative emphasis on the importance of the traditional family unit was embraced by leading Labour politicians, including Tony Blair. He supported the desirability of the two-parent family, and spoke on his tour to South Africa in 1996 of the importance of family life to the creation of 'a decent society'. He argued that it was in the family that people learned the difference between right and wrong, and basic good manners.

- *punishment*: Labour endorsed the need to punish those who broke the law, if necessary by the introduction of legislative penalities for such behaviour. The slogan was, 'Tough on crime, Tough on the causes of crime'. At the 1996 Labour Party Conference, Jack Straw proposed teenage curfews and a crackdown on underage drinking and noisy neighbours. He also proposed action against drug-related crime (which he asserted cost around £1 billion in property stolen by addicts each year to fund their drug habit) which included a pledge to halt the 'vicious circle of addiction and crime'. This included a drug testing and treatment order, administered by probation officers.

THE CONSENSUS ON CRIME AND DISORDER

As the 1997 general election approached, a consensus on crime developed between the government and Labour opposition.

Legislation concerning stalking and the establishment of a register for paedophiles had been proposed to the Conservative Party Conference in October 1996 by the then Home Secretary, Michael Howard. This was part of his law-and-order package to be incorporated into a subsequent Crime Bill. However, these two provisions were initially omitted from the 1996 Queen's speech, on the basis that there was insufficient parliamentary time available to the government for discussing them. It was alternatively proposed that such measures could be the subject of Private Members' Bills. However, the leader of the opposition, Tony Blair, challenged the government to introduce its own legislation to deal with the issues, and pledged that his party would cooperate to put them through the House of Commons. This offer was accepted by the then Prime Minister, John Major.

Both parties also displayed a willingness to take punitive action against the actions of unpopular minority groups. At the beginning of 1997, both parties targeted beggars for such attention.

Political opinion outside of the main parties was restless with what was depicted as a newly-found consensus. The *Observer* on 3 November 1996 remarked that remoralisation backed by repressive legislation demonstrated that there would be no substantive challenge to Britain's system of market capitalism and resultant inequalities: economic and social reform were now 'inadmissible' and the response to crime was that of repression rather than attacking it at its roots.

THE 1998 CRIME AND DISORDER ACT

In office, the Labour approach to crime and disorder revealed a number of differences to the approach adopted by their Conservative predecessors. This was especially obvious in the content of the 1998 Crime and Disorder Act. The Act sought to blend preventive and punitive measures to combat crime. Particular attention was focused on juvenile crime, and the main thrust of the Act was on crime prevention. Whereas Conservative governments had placed considerable emphasis on measures to limit the opportunities for crime to be committed, Labour's approach was far broader, either seeking to prevent persons embarking on crime in the first place, or aiming to stop those who had offended from subsequently re-offending.

Measures to Prevent Crime
The following measures were designed either to protect vulnerable groups from crime or to encourage offenders to change their habits.

- *Anti-Social Behaviour Orders*: these are issued by Magistrates' courts at the request of the police or a local authority. They would be routinely directed at 12–17 year olds (although they could apply to children as young as ten) whose actions caused, or were likely to cause, harassment, alarm or distress. These orders were designed to protect vulnerable groups such as elderly or disabled people, racial minorities, children on their way to and from school, and homosexuals.
- *Sex Offender Orders*: these ban known sex offenders from loitering near schools and playgrounds, and provide supervision orders for sex and violent criminals when they leave prison.
- *Parenting Orders*: these encourage parents to accept responsibility for the behaviour of their children. Such would consist of weekly support/guidance sessions over a three-month period, to help them control unruly children.
- *Child Safety Orders*: these are issued on application of the local authority. They will place a child below the age of ten who is at risk of being involved in crime, under the supervision of a local authority Youth Offender Team or Social Services Department. This is normally for a period of three months.
- *Temporary curfews on children below the age of ten*: local authorities, following consultation with the police and residents, could impose a temporary curfew on children under ten in a specified public area. This effectively bans under-tens from being out alone on the streets in a stipulated geographic area after a designated time. A child found in breach of a curfew order could then be made subject to a Child Safety Order.

Measures to Punish Criminals

The following measures were mainly designed to punish those who committed crime, although some of them were also designed to prevent criminals from subsequently re-offending.

- *Reparation Orders*: these would lead to young offenders making amends for the harm they had done to their victims. Such an order would be granted only after consultation with a local Youth Offender Team, which would then be responsible for supervising the activities contained in the order. Other aspects of what is termed 'restorative justice' (which involved bringing the victim face-to-face with the perpetrator, and his or her family at a mediation conference) were also included within the Act. This 'shaming factor' was advocated on the basis that it had a beneficial impact on preventing juveniles who had broken the law from re-offending.
- *Racially aggravated offences*: measures were introduced to combat racially aggravated assaults, criminal damage, public order offences and harassment.
- *A system of reprimands and warnings to replace the system of police cautions*: repeat cautioning (which was viewed as an ineffective response to juvenile crime) was replaced by a statutory Final Warning Scheme. It was assumed that a youth would be charged for any further offence committed after a Final Warning had been issued.
- *Action Plan Orders*: these were introduced in respect of offenders aged 10–17. These were court orders to provide for an intensive three-month programme to address the causes of offending. This programme would be designed and directed by local authority Youth Offender Teams.
- *Detention and Training Orders*: these comprised of a mixture of 50 per cent detention and 50 per cent community supervision. Detention and Training Orders could be applied to young children at the Home Secretary's discretion.

THE MULTI-AGENCY APPROACH

The perception that the police alone could not tackle crime and that a concerted effort from a wide range of public agencies was required, gave rise to what is termed the 'multi-agency approach'. This was a key feature of community policing methods which were widely introduced by police forces in the 1980s, and this approach was embodied as a key feature of the 1998 legislation. This occurred in two main areas of activity.

First, in connection with local crime prevention schemes. Under the 1998 Act, local authorities were to take the lead role in devising a crime prevention strategy for their areas through what was termed the 'partnership approach'. This entailed placing a statutory duty on police forces and local authorities (together with police authorities, health authorities and probation committees) to work together to develop and implement a strategy for reducing crime and disorder in each district and unitary local authority in England and Wales. This coordinated approach underpinned the broadening of the concept of crime prevention into that of community safety.

The second aspect of the multi-agency approach concerned the youth justice system which had previously been criticised for being fragmented, being composed of a number of agencies (which included the police and social services departments) whose perspectives were different and which sometimes found it difficult to coordinate activities or cooperate effectively. The government thus proposed that local authorities with social services and education responsibilities should be placed under a statutory duty to ensure that youth justice services were provided and coordinated through a Youth Offender Team for their area. Youth Offender Teams should involve professionals from a range of relevant agencies including social workers, probation officers, police officers, education and health authority staff. The government established a Youth Justice Board to coordinate the Youth Justice system at national level.

This approach marked a departure from the policies pursued by previous Conservative governments which, for example, failed to endorse the recommendations of the Morgan report in 1991 which had urged a greater degree of local government involvement in crime prevention policies and expressed support for the multi-agency (or what was termed 'partnership' approach).

ACTION TO COMBAT SOCIAL EXCLUSION

The Labour government sought to tackle the causes of crime through measures which were additional to the 1998 Crime and Disorder Act. For example, the Department of Education and Employment is introducing mandatory lessons in citizenship to be provided in all schools from 2002. Social exclusion was also identified as a key factor underlying crime, and the government addressed this in the following initiatives:

'Welfare to Work'

This guaranteed the opportunity to work or train for every young person over the age of 18 who had been out of work for more than six months, and for young people leaving prison. A prototype scheme, the New Deal for Lone Parents, was also launched. This embraced a package of aid including training, job searching and after-school care, designed to aid the transition from welfare to work.

The Social Exclusion Unit

This would develop programmes to promote social improvement and encourage local initiatives to create jobs. Some of its proposals to achieve this (such as the suggestion in 1999 that teenage girls should be offered contraceptives without their parents' knowledge, in order to reduce the high number of teenage preganancies) were politically contentious.

'New Deal for Communities'

This was launched in September 1998, and sought to tackle poverty in the poorest urban areas. The measures included:

- targeting a small area with special resources
- developing a regeneration programme in which the private, community and the voluntary sectors work in partnership
- better coordinating of the activities pursued by various government departments.

Areas of acute social need might qualify for Single Regeneration Bids (which were designed to aid regeneration), and 18 Action Teams were established in particularly disadvantaged neighbourhoods.

Family Support

Aid was directed at families, children and schools in order to stop children drifting into crime. This might be achieved by seeking to tackle family breakdown (which had been viewed as a major cause of crime), and school initiatives to cut truancy, drug and substance abuse, bullying and the risk of exclusion. Intensified aid to children thought to be at risk of offending, was provided. In 1999 the government provided £200 million of intensive nursery schemes to supplement the Sure Start programme. These schemes were provided in high crime areas, and were directed at children whose upbringing led them to be perceived as potential future offenders. The aim of such programmes was to teach young children how to think ahead and organise their lives. It was anticipated that that this would produce observable benefits by the time the child reached ten, measured by indicators which included improved school behaviour and achievement, and fewer signs of criminality.

Improvement of educational standards in urban areas

This approach included the injection of additional aid to improve the educational attainment of children attending inner-city comprehensive schools. Some of this aid would be spent on providing 'masterclasses' at specialist schools for the ablest children, and the number of specialist and beacon schools would be greatly expanded. 'Pupil advocates' would be appointed to aid the low achievers and raise their expectations. Although this approach could be viewed as a desire to improve educational standards for all children, there arose the possibility that this policy would intensify social divisions by aiding educational attainment (and ultimately social mobility) for a gifted minority, while intensifying perceptions of social disadvantage for the remainder. Additionally, Achievement Grants were made available to aid the educational attainment of ethnic minority pupils, who were at risk of underperforming.

ADVANTAGES OF LABOUR'S APPROACH TO CRIME AND DISORDER

The main advantages of the government's approach can be summarised as follows:

- *The approach towards crime prevention was more comprehensive than that of Conservative governments*: the Conservative emphasis on measures to limit the opportunities for crime to be committed (a particular objective of the National Crime Prevention Agency established in 1995) was developed by Labour into a broader set of measures. These were designed either to prevent persons from embarking on crime, or from reoffending.
- *It ended an over-reliance on retribution*: the belief that stiff punishment was sufficient to deter criminal behaviour gave way to a balanced response, which blended prevention and rehabilitation with punitive measures.
- *It sought to address the social causes of crime*: the Labour government positively responded to arguments put forward by bodies such as the Audit Commission, which argued in 1996 that the lack of jobs, adequate nursery education and family centres to help young isolated mothers, contributed to the level of youth crime.
- *It placed the multi-agency approach on a statutory footing*: Labour sought to provide enhanced coordination between various agencies in response to crime. Additionally, Labour's proposals placed local government in the 'driving seat'. Earlier initiatives involving multi-agency approaches had sometimes floundered because they were perceived as police-driven.
- *It speeded up the operations of the youth justice system*: the government proposed to reduce the time taken to deal with young offenders. It focused on speeding up the youth justice system, arguing that delays angered, frustrated and distressed victims, while doing nothing to help young offenders.
- *It made juvenile offenders (and their parents) take responsibility for their actions*: this aspect of the government's reforms sought to make young offenders and their parents take responsibility for their actions, so that young offenders would learn a valuable moral lesson and take the first step towards rehabilitation. This was designed to end what has been described as the 'excuse culture' of the youth justice system, which implied that young people were not responsible for their behaviour.

DISADVANTAGES OF LABOUR'S APPROACH TO CRIME AND DISORDER

The approach adopted, however, has been subject to a number of criticisms which are discussed below:

- *The approach adopted towards juveniles may be too severe*: the development of a separate system of youth justice was based on the belief that children were not totally responsible for their criminal actions. The Conservative belief that children should be accountable for their criminality was sustained in Labour's removal of the common law presumption of 'doli incapax', whereby the prosecution had to prove that children aged 10-13 knew the difference between right and wrong. This reform would enable children who ought to be prosecuted to appear in court.

- *The rights of accused persons are insufficiently protected*: Anti Social Behaviour Orders and Child Safety Orders are issued on the civil law test of the balance of probabilities, rather than the criminal proof test of beyond reasonable doubt. Juveniles under such sanctions will not have any right to cross-examine prosecution witnesses.
- *The new multi-agency arrangements may pose a number of administrative problems*: the proposals require an enhanced degree of coordination of local authority services, which had traditionally been hindered by departmentalism. Additional problems are faced by police forces, which have to liaise with a number of different local authorities.
- *Resource implications*: the proposals in the consultation papers possessed considerable resource implications in terms of staff training, staff time, and the development of new programmes and bail support facilities. It was not clear, however, that the government was willing to provide the funding required for these new arrangements.

THE END OF CONSENSUS?

Although there are considerable differences in the approach adopted by the Labour government towards crime and disorder after 1997 (most notably addressing the social causes of crime and in the emphasising of prevention rather than retribution), some similarities in the approach of both parties remained.

Retribution
The emphasis on retribution was maintained: the size of the prison population continued to grow in the early years of the Labour government, from 63,799 in November 1997 to 66,100 in November 1998. In the *Guardian* on 31 March 1998, the journalist Simon Hoggart referred to a 'new consensus of untrammelled toughness' and a 'blame the culprit' culture.

The Role of the Family
As with the Conservative Party, Labour continued to stress the importance of the traditional family unit: in January 1999 the Home Secretary, Jack Straw, suggested that more teenage mothers should give their children up for adoption. He asserted that too many 'well-meaning but misguided' social workers encouraged young mothers with no financial or emotional stability to keep their babies, who often ended up in care at a later stage. However, this view ignored the fact that many very young children being looked after by local authorities

were *not* from teenage single mothers, and that many of these were successfully returned to their families.

Prominent attention placed on the needs of society

The need to protect society from the consequences of crime through the use of punitive measures was especially apparent in:

- Jack Straw's announcement in February 1999 of plans to lock up potentially violent psychopaths even if they had committed no crime
- the support given by the government to a Private Member's Bill in 1999 which sought to establish a single blacklist of suspected paedophiles, which any potential employer working with children would be obliged to consult.

Such suggestions seemed contrary to the emphasis placed on human rights elsewhere in the government's political programme.

THE DEPOLITICISATION OF CRIME?

Regarding crime as a key political issue can be criticised. Parties may base their policies on what they *perceive* to be the mood of the general public, rather than being based on more rational and dispassionate sentiments designed to cure a social evil. This was especially displayed in the early 1990s, when the Conservative and Labour parties sought to outbid each other for being 'tough' in their approach to law and order.

This situation prompted Lord Ackner to urge the creation of an Advisory Council on Criminal Justice. This would consist of an independent body of experts drawn from different professions, who would advise governments contemplating changes in criminal law and the criminal justice system. It would effectively depoliticise the response to crime.

THE STYLE OF POLICING SINCE 1979

The desire to adopt a tough approach to crime after 1979 was reflected in the move towards a more paramilitary style of policing. This involved the police reacting aggressively in situations when law and order was threatened. Developments of this policy included the routine arming of the police (which typically involved the deployment of specialist, armed units available as an instant response capacity to serious crime), the use of batons rather than the traditional truncheon, and the introduction of pepper and CS sprays. Zero tolerance policing was compatible with many aspects of this new approach to policing society.

ZERO TOLERANCE POLICING

This method of policing has been adopted in American cities such as New York, where it seems to have a major impact on the level of crime. Its main features are to concentrate on specific geographic areas, and within them to take strict action so that:

- *all forms of crime become the subject of police activity*: it was assumed that police intervention against even the most minor of crimes, could prevent the perpetrators moving on to more serious forms of criminal activity. The aim, therefore, is to nip criminal activity in the bud and prevent it from developing into more serious types of deviant behaviour.

- *the police assume a tough response to criminal activity*: eg, in Middlesbrough, zero tolerance policing has involved activities such as high profile raids on the homes of suspected criminals, and the use of road blocks and stop-and-search operations. Tough action is associated with paramilitary policing methods, and includes the willingness to use weaponry such as CS spray. On 29 September 1998, the *Guardian* reported that CS spray was used 600 times in one year in Cleveland, the highest in any constabulary area.

The main driving force behind zero tolerance policing is to reduce crime, especially burglary, as evidenced in crime statistics. There are, however, problems:

Departure from minimum force
Although such developments could be justified by the need for police officers to defend themselves when encountering violent crime or behaviour, they pose the danger of police weaponry being routinely deployed in an *offensive* rather than *defensive* fashion, thus departing from the traditional principle of minimum force. This issue was raised in connection with the fatal shooting of James Ashley by Sussex police in 1998. This event resulted in the police authority temporarily suspending its chief constable in 1999, and in the officer who fired the fatal shot being charged with murder and manslaughter.

Public acceptability
The emphasis on law enforcement downplays other crucial aspects of police work (such as its service role) which are important in creating good relationships between police and the public. Additionally, there is the danger that the public may react adversely to tough policing methods if these are deemed to constitute an overreaction on the part of the police. Errors of judgement are most likely to arise when officers are 'psyched up' to be tough on the streets, and result in friction between police and public which has been a significant factor in urban disorders since 1980.

Police work becomes result driven

Zero tolerance policing seeks to demonstrate success in the war against crime. This sometimes leads to the use of improper practices, in the belief that the end justified the means. Thus in October 1997, two Middlesbrough officers were suspended after allegations that prisoners in police cells had been given heroin in return for confessions. As a result, several Crown Court cases collapsed because police evidence was deemed to be unsafe, and a major enquiry was initiated by the Police Complaints Authority into corruption and malpractice in the Cleveland force.

Uncertain effectiveness

Evidence suggests that zero tolerance policing reduces crime in selected areas in the short term by displacing it to others. The success of such a strategy in New York might have been due to the large increase in police officers rather than the tactic of zero tolerance.

Provisions of the 1998 Crime and Disorder Act such as Anti Social Behaviour Orders and child curfews are compatible with zero tolerance policing. However, the concentration on the symptoms rather than the causes of crime, and the reactive nature of zero tolerance policing did not fit easily alongside the preventive aspects of the 1998 legislation and other related initiatives pursued by the Labour government. At the 1998 Labour Party Conference, the Prime Minister Tony Blair proposed the introduction of 'order maintenance' into 25 crime 'hot spot' areas throughout Britain. This included a more targeted use of police patrols, based on the belief that random patrols were largely ineffective in deterring crime or catching criminals. This blended the reactive aspects of zero tolerance with crime prevention.

SUMMARY

After reading this Chapter, you should be able to evaluate:

- the importance of crime as a political issue
- the strengths and weaknesses of official crime statistics as indicators of the level of crime in society
- the approaches adopted by the Conservative Party between 1979 and 1997 to combat crime
- the policies adopted by the Labour Party while in opposition and in government after 1997 to combat crime, highlighting the similarities and differences in their approach with that of the Conservative Party
- the content of the 1998 Crime and Disorder Act and other Labour measures designed to tackle to social roots of crime
- the advantages and disadvantages of zero tolerance policing.

STUDY GUIDES

Revision Hints

You should appreciate the way in which questions which deal with crime are likely to evolve. Until 1997 the main approach was likely to require an assessment of policies pursued by Conservative governments in this area, in particular seeking to highlight the inconsistencies in the approach pursued. In the years immediately after 1997 the main thrust of questions was concerned with a comparative analysis of the Conservative and Labour parties' approach to crime, seeking an assessment of the similarities and, most importantly, the differences in the approach pursued by the Labour government after 1997. Future questions are likely to increasingly emphasise the philosophy of Labour's approach to crime.

Exam Hints

Answering short questions on crime and the political parties

1   Identify two examples of policies pursued by a Conservative government to combat crime which they subsequently abandoned.

This question is concerned with U-turns in the approach adopted by Conservative governments to crime between 1979 and 1997. Examples of this might be the reversal of the 'short, sharp shock' for juvenile offenders in the 1980s; or the move away from the 1991 Criminal Justice Act's emphasis on non-custodial sentences for the less serious offenders, to the more widespread use of imprisonment, especially after the 1992 general election. To answer this question you need to identify two examples, fully explaining the content and underlying philosophy of the approach that was initially embarked upon, how this differed from previous policies in that area, and in what ways (and when) the new policy was subsequently abandoned. Although the question is primarily concerned with discussion and description of policy changes, a brief statement as to why the policy was altered would aid the answer.

Answering Essay Questions on Crime and the Political Parties

2   To what extent do the policies introduced by the Labour government after 1997 to deal with rising crime differ from those pursued by previous Conservative governments?

To answer this question you should identify the key approaches adopted by the Labour government in its crime and disorder legislation, and other policies designed to tackle the social roots of crime, and contrast these with the policies adopted by earlier Conservative governments. You would not be expected to pick out every key difference, but to provide a knowledgeable discussion of perhaps two or three main trends. Such might include Labour's endorsement of the multi-agency approach to crime prevention, the way in which their crime prevention policies were more sophisticated than those of previous Conservative governments, or the attempt to tackle the social causes of crime rather than rely on stiff punishments to deter such behaviour. Examples of the actions of Conservative governments should be used to draw out the differences in the approach of both parties. Do not forget, however, that there are also similarities in the approach adopted: this might be illustrated by the apparent consensus towards the end of the 1992-1997 Conservative government, on the continued emphasis placed by the Labour government on the family as the social unit to teach children right from wrong, or on the importance attached to retribution (which was evidenced by the size of the prison population).

Practice Questions

1 Discuss *one* similarity and *one* difference in the approach adopted by Conservative and Labour governments to combat crime in the 1990s.
2 'Tough on crime; tough on the causes of crime'. To what extent have policies pursued by Labour governments to combat crime reflected this approach since 1997?

3

PROTEST, DISSENT AND PUBLIC DISORDER

Introduction

As with crime, widespread outbreaks of public disorder may also undermine a government's credibility. Injuries to persons and damage to property may imply that a government lacks the ability to protect its citizens adequately, and widespread dissent may threaten its capacity to govern the country effectively. The image of industrial unrest which was spiralling out of control in 1978/1979 in the so-called 'winter of discontent' was an important factor in the general election victory of the Conservative Party in 1979.

Key Points

This chapter will discuss the following key issues:

- the main examples of protest, dissent and public disorder which have occurred since 1979
- reasons why extra-parliamentary political activity formed an important aspect of the politics of this period.
- the causes of inner-city disorders since 1980
- the legislative responses to public disorder.

THE ARTICULATION OF PROTEST AND DISSENT

Extra-parliamentary political activity is intimately associated with methods of protest and dissent. This section examines the main ways in which protest can be expressed and dissent voiced.

DEMONSTRATIONS

In 1985 the Conservative government's white paper, Review of Public Order Law, stated that the rights of peaceful protest and assembly were 'amongst our fundamental freedoms' and were 'numbered among the touchstones which distinguish a free society from a totalitarian one'. Thus in a liberal democracy the ability to take to the streets and participate in activities such as demonstrations or rallies in order to air one's opinions, constitutes an important avenue of political expression. These activities are usually designed to mobilise public opinion in support of a specific policy or cause, which places pressure on the government to adopt this course of action.

Since 1979, they have been used in connection with a number of causes, which include opposition to policies on race such as the National Front and British National Party, and to protest against specific items of government policy including the introduction of poll tax (which came into effect in England and Wales in 1990), and the 1994 Criminal Justice and Public Order legislation. Additionally, demonstrations have sometimes been used to influence the activities of the private sector.

DISORDER AT DEMONSTRATIONS AND RALLIES

Most demonstrations and rallies are peaceful events. However, disorder has often occurred at them. Violence may occur at such events when opposing groups clash. This has been a feature of demonstrations connected with the politics of race when members of the National Front and British National party were physically opposed by groups such as the Anti Nazi League. Attempts by the police to keep warring groups apart frequently places them in the firing line. In October 1993 an anti-racist demonstration directed at the British National Party at Welling, South East London, resulted in the injury of 21 police and 41 demonstrators. The following month 200 police officers and 50 members of the public were injured at a protest march in the same vicinity.

Violence at demonstrations also arises when extremist groups seek to use an occasion when large numbers of people are on the streets to further their own political ends. This may take the form of provoking police action in order to depict the state and its agencies as brutal, thereby bringing them into public disrepute. This was a contributing factor to the disorder which occured at the Trafalgar Square anti-poll tax rally in 1990, and the rally organised by the Coalition against the Criminal Justice Bill in 1994 at Hyde Park in London. At this latter event the *Guardian* on 10 October 1994 reported that the police were pelted with missiles which included beer cans filled with sand, CS gas cannisters and blazing lumps of wood and bottles. The police responded by charging the demonstrators, sometimes deploying mounted police.

DIRECT ACTION

The desire to influence public opinion by taking a cause to 'the streets' is one feature of protest and dissent since 1945. Additionally some groups have sought to further their cause through the use of various forms of direct action. The objectives sought by direct action are broad, ranging from local concerns (such as securing traffic restrictions on busy roads), to the repudiation of the entire political system, and the promotion of revolution. The tactics of direct action are also varied, ranging from non-violent methods such as civil disobedience, to actions involving the considerable use of force. The activities by some animal welfare groups, especially the militant Animal Liberation Front, have been likened to acts of terrorism. In 1995 a number of incendiary devices were sent to farmers involved in the live animal export trade, and in 1998 activists of the Animal Liberation Front released thousands of mink from fur farms in Hampshire and Staffordshire.

DEMONSTRATION BY THE ANIMAL LIBERATION FRONT

Direct action and public disorder

Direct action and the State's response to it have sometimes resulted in disorder. Attempts to prevent motorway construction during the 1990s, for example, often involved protestors waging pitched battles with police, bailiffs and security guards to avoid eviction from camps and tree houses. Allegations of violence were made by both sides of the dispute and particular criticism was directed against security guards who, unlike the police, do not operate in accordance with any disciplinary code. It was alleged that unnecessary violence was used in evicting protesters from tree houses by methods which failed to display acceptable standards of care and safety towards the protestors.

The campaign by groups such as Compassion in World Farming against the export of British cattle to Europe for use in the veal trade, resulted in major public disorders at Brightlingsea and Shoreham, and the death of a protestor, Jill Phipps, outside Coventry Airport in February 1995. Disorder occurred when protestors seeking to prevent lorries taking animals to ports and airports clashed with the police, whose role was to prevent obstructions to the highway. The *Guardian* on 21 April 1995 reported how on the previous day at Brightlingsea, police officers 'came under a hail of missiles, including bottles, beer cans, coins, stones – and eggs apparently injected with a paint or purple chemical'. An officer was stabbed in August 1995 whilst policing a protest. Counter-claims of overly aggressive policing to clear the roads for lorries were made by residents of Brightlingsea; they objected to the use of long batons by the police, and the wearing of balaclavas which they perceived to be intimidating. A thousand residents took to the streets to protest against police tactics.

Civil disobedience
Civil disobedience is a difficult term to define precisely. It is an act undertaken by a person in his or her capacity as a citizen under government, entailing disobedience which is both passive and non-violent. Civil disobedience is associated with tactics which include vigils, mass sit-ins or trespass. The aims of such tactics are to draw public attention to the objectives of the group and establish a sense of solidarity amongst the members of the organisation.

INDUSTRIAL DISPUTES

Industrial disputes constitute an important tactic of protest and dissent. Although such episodes may be primarily concerned with 'bread and butter' issues of pay and better working conditions, they may also have a political aspect. It is in this latter sense that strike action can be viewed as a form of political activity. This situation may occur for reasons which include:

- *government policies triggering unrest*: government economic policy has been the cause of numerous industrial disputes since the 1970s, when controls were introduced to combat inflation. This meant that workers seeking improved pay and conditions had to confront government policy rather than their employers. In the 1980s, the Conservative endorsement of the free market resulted in high unemployment. Those affected by such developments sometimes resorted to industrial action. One significant example of this was the miners' strike of 1984-5.

- *challenge to capitalism*: some on the left of the political spectrum endorse industrial militancy to advance working class interests, rather than conventional political activity. One such group, the syndicalists, asserted that strikes sharpened the class struggle and the participation by workers in strikes promoted feelings of solidarity and community. These sentiments would result in a revolutionary seizure of the means of production by a general strike.

MARXIST AND LIBERAL ANALYSIS OF STRIKES

Marxists view all strike activity as political since it poses a threat to profits. They assert that in a capitalist society, the key role of the State is to ensure that conditions exist to attain the accumulation of capital. This requires it to manage the conflict which they believe will inevitably arise between employers and their exploited workers. Thus the nature of State intervention in industrial disputes is viewed to be both consistent and one-sided, giving rise to an accusation that bodies such as the police and support owners or managers, oppose actions undertaken by trade unionists.

Liberals, however, believe that owners and workers share a common interest since both benefit from profitable businesses. They also believe that the maintenance of law and public order is in the interests of all and not merely the economically powerful. Liberals assert that it is legitimate for the State to intervene to defend individual liberties (such as the right to work during a strike) when these are threatened by intimidatory behaviour.

Industrial disputes and public disorder

The number of working days lost through industrial action on a yearly average basis was 12.9 million in the 1970s and 7.2 million in the 1980s. However, during the early 1990s, the level of industrial militancy began to fall, and the figure of 278,000 working days lost through industrial disputes in 1994 was the lowest since 1981. Although this figure showed signs of increasing in the mid-1990s, there was some evidence to suggest that the British had 'kicked the habit of going on strike'.

Industrial disputes have posed major threats to public order since 1979. This is most likely to arise when such events require police intervention, designed either to uphold the law (eg by keeping roads open), or to safeguard the rights of those wishing to work during an industrial dispute, who may be prevented from doing so by intimidatory or violent actions on picket lines. The police thus become the subject of attack, either because they are viewed as the personification of a state whose policies are seen as unwise or unjust, or because their attempt to uphold public tranquillity results in accusations of police partiality for the views of one of the two 'sides' present at a specific event. In these cases the violence of those engaged in industrial disputes is frequently directed against the police who may respond aggressively.

The 'Battle of Orgreave' in 1984 during the miners' dispute was an extreme example of disorder involving strikers and the police. It was followed by other events at which violence occurred, especially in connection with News International's dispute with the print unions at Wapping in 1986–1987.

ARTHUR SCARGILL ARRESTED DURING MINERS' STRIKE, ORGREAVE, MAY 1984

COUNTER CULTURAL FORMS OF PROTEST

People who feel alienated from society may display dissent through activities described as 'counter cultural'. Counter culture embraces a wide range of actions which are frequently associated with young people. These actions may be described as political in the sense they are based upon:

- *the rejection of society*: counter cultural protest rejects the norms and values on which the existing social order is based. A particular feature of this during the 1990s has been opposition to materialism.
- *empowerment*: counter cultural protest is often coupled with attempts to develop alternative lifestyles. It seeks to enable its practitioners to live their lives according to their own rules and standards, thus effecting a small redistribution of power in their favour.

Counter cultural protest and public disorder

Typically counter cultural protest involves an attack on conventional behaviour (delivered in various ways including music and literature), which is often designed to shock 'respectable' society. In the 1990s, large numbers of youths adopted rave as their culture. This blended the 1970s festival movement with urban youth culture and was particularly associated with participation at events at which loud music was played. Counter culture may involve the illegal use of drugs: eg, hippies made use of psychedelic drugs, and the more recent rave (or acid house) phenomenon has been linked to the use of ecstasy.

'New Age Travellers' (a description applied to a diverse range of groups who share a common desire for freedom and a rejection of the State) are associated with lifestyles which contravene established patterns of social behaviour. They have frequently been at the centre of violence, arising from police actions to prevent them occupying common land or when evicting them from private land. In June 1985, 1,000 officers drawn from five police forces intercepted a convey of travellers on the border of Hampshire and Wiltshire. English Heritage and the National Trust obtained injunctions to bar them from their land, and the police herded them into a field where they, their vans and buses were subjected to action which was subsequently described by the ITN journalist Ken Sabido as 'the most brutal treatment of people I've witnessed in my entire career as a journalist'. In total, 420 travellers were arrested in the 'battle of the beanfield' which is generally regarded to have instigated grass roots environmentalism.

EXPLANATIONS OF PROTEST AND DISSENT

The various forms of protest and dissent discussed above have constituted an important aspect of political activity after 1979. This section examines some key explanations to account for the use of such tactics.

FORMAL ACCESS TO A STATE'S DECISION-MAKING PROCESS

Formal access to a state's decision-making machinery is provided by institutionalised channels, whereby citizens (either individually or acting in groups) are 'plugged into' the policy-making process. The extent of formal access (ie, the number of 'sockets' which citizens or groups can 'plug into') is influenced by factors which include the nature of a state's political system, the extent of decentralisation, the operations of the bureaucracy, and the opportunities possessed by the general public (through devices such as referendums) to place their demands onto the political agenda. Formal political access is limited in the UK. It is a unitary state in which political power is centralised. The working practices of the bureaucracy tend to encourage formal links with a relatively small number of insider pressure groups, while the concept of the sovereignty of Parliament has traditionally been used to prevent the regular or widespread usage of referendums or other devices associated with direct democracy.

One consequence of this situation is that groups which are denied formal access may use methods of protest and dissent to voice their political concerns. The nature of formal access to Britain's decision-making machinery is not static however, and changes to it may influence the extent of extra-parliamentary activity. Two of these factors are discussed below.

The Corporate State

Trade unions traditionally used the strike weapon to advance their demands. However, during the 1960s, British trade unions succeeded in cultivating a close working relationship with central government and business organisations. Policy was subsequently hammered out in the forum of the National Economic Development Council (NEDDY) in which members of the government, leading trade unionists and employers effectively determined major issues of industrial and economic policy. Such structures potentially reduced the level of industrial unrest, by securing greater economic equality in return for improved economic performance. Thus, States which developed corporatist bargaining structures including national associations of capital and labour and top governmental officials, tended to secure a degree of insulation from outbreaks of protest and violence. However, the abandonment of this corporate approach by Conservative governments after 1979 and their antagonism towards trade unions promoted protest, particularly in the form of industrial unrest. The miners' dispute of 1984–5 was a major example of union-directed protest.

The European Union

The UK's membership of the European Union provided new points of formal political access. Groups could bypass national governments and seek their objectives through the EU, especially when their own government was hostile to their aims. The interests of British trade unions were reflected in developments such as the Social Chapter. The restrictions placed on trade unions by Conservative governments after 1979 also served to enhance the importance of EU institutions, such as the European Court of Justice as a defence of trade union and workers' interests. However, although the EU may restrict the need for protest and dissent on some occasions, protest may be stimulated by the existence of supranational institutions, which bring together similar groups operating in a number of countries. The development of social movements concerned with altering moral behaviour across national frontiers, has had a positive effect on British extra-parliamentary organisations, especially those concerned with the protection of the environment.

SOCIAL MOVEMENTS

The traditional role undertaken by pressure groups to promote political change in Britain has more recently been supplemented by organisations termed 'social movements'. These are associated with the leftwing of the political spectrum but have substituted the traditional Marxist goal of overthrowing capitalism by a working class revolution, with a range of direct action tactics which seek to transform society by redefining social values and thus culturally undermine this economic system.

The Environmental movement is an important example of a contemporary social movement. It has succeeded in bringing together a range of groups engaged in counter cultural protest (such as New Age Travellers), and those opposed to hunting, live animal exports, motorway construction and pollution. These seemingly disparate, single-issue bodies (ie, bodies whose aims seem contrasting) are united by a social vision which rejects the culture of advanced capitalist society. All stand opposed to what they view as an alliance of developers, business, the construction industry and government. They have utilised tactics of protest and direct action to project an alternative vision to a modern industrial society, which emphasises environmental considerations over the pursuit of wealth and profit. All are concerned with human damage to the planet, and are opposed to materialism and consumerism.

THE OPERATIONS OF THE POLITICAL SYSTEM

A wide range of formal and informal factors influence the ability of individuals to adopt methods of protest or dissent. These include:

- *developments in communication*: television has made it possible for groups such as Greenpeace to reach a wide audience, through the use of spectacular forms of direct action. Further developments including the internet, desk-top publishing and local television and radio stations may enhance the opportunity for groups engaged in protest and direct action to organise or obtain publicity.
- *the extent of support for conventional political activity*: popular perceptions of the authority and credibility of the government, and support for the operations of a liberal democratic political system, may influence protest and dissent. In Britain, allegations associated with 'sleaze' in the 1990s may have an adverse effect on the level of support which citizens give to conventional political activity.

This section concentrates on three key factors associated with the operations of the political system in Britain since 1945, which may serve to stimulate protest and dissent.

The electoral system

The first-past-the-post electoral system may encourage groups to utilise protest and dissent for two main reasons.

1 It encourages the formation of 'broad church' parties, which make it difficult for single-issue groups to make much headway within the conventional political system. However, the opposite of this argument is not consistently true: proportional representation does not always limit the level of protest and dissent. In the former state of West Germany, for example, a number of strong social movements emerged during the 1970s. They believed that too close an association with one particular political party hampered the group's effectiveness, either by tying it too closely to the political fortunes of that party, or by making it difficult for the group to work with other political parties which might form the government.

2 It tends to distort the verdict of the voters, often giving the largest party a disproportionate share of seats in the House of Commons. This aids control by the executive and may result in opposition tactics being voiced by extra-parliamentary methods. The dominance of the Conservative party between 1979 and 1997 encouraged such activity by groups who despaired of attaining their objectives through conventional political activity. A more recent example of this situation occurred on 1 March 1998, when a demonstration organised by the Countryside Alliance in London attracted in excess of 250,000 people. Many rural Britons became anxious that their way of life was under threat because of the dominant position of the Labour Party, which had traditionally been identified with the concerns of the urban working class. The protestors sought to assert the concerns of rural Britain through extra-parliamentary means, and in particular to voice their opposition at a Bill which proposed to outlaw the hunting of foxes and other wild animals with dogs (put forward by a backbench Labour MP, Michael Foster).

The party system

The tendency of individuals and groups to seek political change through the established political parties is affected by a number of factors. The parties generally concentrate on a narrow range of policies, and exclude consideration of other issues. Examples of this include immigration and, more recently, animal welfare. The extent to which a party's decision-making machinery can be influenced by the opinions of its members, may also influence the support given to conventional political activity. Parties whose policy-making processes are centralised and relatively unaffected by grassroots opinion, are unlikely to serve as vehicles for minority opinions which may thus be expressed through extra-parliamentary methods.

Since 1970, the strength of the British party system has been affected by partisan and class dealignment. This has benefited issue-based politics. This may help to explain the increased support obtained by single-issue pressure groups and social movements in recent times.

The Labour Party and radical politics

The failure of parties on the left of the political spectrum to advance radical political and social reform and instead to pursue consensus politics, may encourage the growth of extra-parliamentary activity. The domination of British politics after 1979 by the Conservative Party had a significant impact on the policies of the Labour Party, and the ultimate development of a new political consensus underpinned by support for the free market. This provided political space for movements which were motivated by an alternative vision of society, and helped to explain the increased influence of 'people politics' during the 1990s.

URBAN DISORDER AND ITS CAUSES

Urban disorder, or rioting, occurred at relatively regular intervals between 1980 (commencing with the disorder which occurred in the St Paul's area of Bristol) and 1997. As with crime, there are two broad perspectives from which such events can be viewed.

1 *The Moral Failings of the Individual.* This perspective viewed rioting as an activity associated with moral *depravation*. The riots were explained by factors which included the breakdown of the family unit, the decline of religion, and the loss of respect for authority. This viewpoint held that disorders were underpinned by greed and wickedness, in which a criminal rather than a political motive was apparent.

2 *The Failings of Society.* This view asserted that rioting was designed to secure reforms, to benefit people who believed that their needs were being neglected or ignored by government. Disorders were thus seen as a cry for help from those who were suffering from various forms of *deprivation* (such as unemployment, poor housing, racial discrimination, an inadequate education system, and deficient leisure facilities). This perspective suggested that the participants had clear motives and objectives guiding their behaviour: urban disorders were seen as political activities, an extreme form of protest and dissent.

Studies of urban disorder in Britain between 1980 and 1997 cited a number of arguments alleging that the operations of society failed groups of people who subsequently engaged in disorderly activities. The main ones are discussed below.

POLITICAL MARGINALISATION

This explanation suggested that the conventional political system failed to cater for the needs of certain sections of society, who were thus compelled to take more drastic action to ensure that governments sat up and took notice of them. Unlike contemporary protest (which is not totally identified with any specific social class), urban disorders typically involved those at the bottom of the social ladder, who despaired of conventional political activity to solve their problems. In this sense, these events were depicted (in the words of two American sociologists, Bachrach and Baratz) as the 'ballot boxes of the poor'.

RACIAL DISCRIMINATION AND SOCIAL DISADVANTAGE

Ethnic minorities constituted one important section of society whose needs were not being adequately catered for by the conventional political system. Most of the disorders which occurred in the 1980s were in multi-ethnic areas; members of such communities experienced a range of social disadvantages, especially unemployment, which were underpinned by racial discrimination. This view suggested that riots were a collective form of political action by ethnic minority groups, at which they vented their outrage against an unjust society and sought, through violence, to secure reforms. However, this explanation requires some qualification. White people as well as black people were participated in such disorders in the 1980s, and in the 1990s the profile of areas where riots occurred, altered. Serious disorders occurred in places such as Tyneside's Meadow Well Estate and Salford, which were inhabited almost exclusively by white people.

The emergence of an *underclass* links events in the 1980s to those of the 1990s. This consists of people who were excluded from the operations of the market economy, introduced during the 1980s. Initially the impact of recession was experienced by semi-skilled and unskilled workers belonging to racial minorities (and in this sense, therefore, race was relevant as an explanantion of such events). By the 1990s, however, recession had become deeper and affected white as well as black members of the working class. This view suggested that social and economic (as opposed to racial) injustices were major underpinnings of urban disorder after 1980, although factors such as poor employment prospects and bad housing could be compounded by racial prejudice, discrimination and violence. These factors were deemed to have been important in radicalising Asian youths involved in the riots in the Manningham area of Bradford in 1995.

POLICING POLICIES IN INNER CITY AREAS: THE SCARMAN REPORT

Poor relationships between police and ethnic minority communities were regarded as key explanations for the occurrence of urban disorders in the early 1980s. A report following the 1981 riots in Brixton by the North Kensington Law Centre asserted that many people in the area, especially young black people, believed that the police 'cannot be trusted, harass people for no reason, often arresting them for offences they have not committed and that following arrest will assault them and humiliate them if the opportunity arises'. Police misbehaviour towards members of ethnic minority communities was stated to include passport raids and checks, unwarranted interventions in political and social life, poor treatment of those held in custody and inadequate responses to racial attacks. It was further alleged that the police complaints system worked less satisfactorily for black persons that it did for whites.

Stop-and-search powers were particularly criticised. These were allegedly used in a discriminatory fashion, underlaid by police stereotyping of persons and communities. This resulted in a form of policing deemed oppressive and unjust by those on the receiving end.

ALLEGATIONS OF ABUSE OF POWER

Evidence supplied to the Scarman inquiry revealed that in the London Borough of Lambeth in 1979 and 1980 there were:

- 14,109 stops of black persons
- 26,004 stops of white persons
- 4, 305 stops of other groups (including Asians)

Black persons thus accounted for 32 per cent of all police stops, and additionally constituted 35 per cent of all arrests in the Borough (2,458 out of 6,952) in this two-year period.

These figures are taken from Martin Kettle and Lucy Hodge, *Uprising*! (London: Pan Books, 1982).

The belief that policing methods contributed to public disorder in 1981 was given official recognition in Lord Scarman's report into these events, particularly those in Brixton. Scarman's investigation was an enquiry constituted under the 1964 Police Act, thus the bulk of his report concentrated on the policing of the affected areas and resulted in the introduction of a wide range of initiatives designed to improve police–public relationships. Particular attention was devoted to multi-ethnic communities. Scarman noted that the police had failed to adapt themselves adequately to operate in such areas, and that existing training arrangements were inadequate to prepare officers for policing a multi-racial society. To address such problems he suggested:

- The modification of police training programmes to incorporate an increased emphasis on community relations.
- The composition of police forces should become more reflective of the society they served: Lord Scarman's report identified only 132 black police officers serving in the Metropolitan Police (0.5 per cent of the strength of that force). However, he rejected a quota system or the lowering of entry standards as mechanisms to achieve this ideal.

- Racially prejudiced or discriminatory behaviour should become a specific disciplinary offence which, if substantiated, would normally lead to dismissal from the police service.
- Amendments to the procedures involved in handling complaints made against the police including the introduction of a conciliation process for minor issues.

The police service was receptive to the introduction of reforms in the wake of the 1980 and 1981 disorders. Some developments (such as community policing initiatives designed to bring the police and public closer together) preceded the Scarman report, and received increased impetus in the early 1980s. Increased attention was placed on interviewing procedures and the content of police training programmes, to ensure that officers, and particularly recruits, were sensitive to the background of residents of multi-ethnic urban areas. Vigorous attempts were also made to increase the number of police officers drawn from minority communities. Further reforms were contained in the 1984 Police and Criminal Evidence Act, which is discussed in Chapter 6.

However, although many disorders were triggered by police actions, it does not necessarily mean that policing was the root cause of the events which then unfolded. The anger vented towards the police could arise from the fact that they are a physical embodiment of a society whose operations are deemed unfair by those who riot. Nonetheless, police actions have some bearing on the disorders which occurred after 1979. The police who work in deprived neighbourhoods can make living conditions for the residents even more intolerable if they deploy methods deemed as overbearing or coercive. The May 1992 riots in the American city of Los Angeles (which occurred following the acquittal by a jury of police officers who had brutally beaten a black motorist, Rodney King) indicated that police abuse of power is viewed as an important symbol of an unjust society.

EXAMPLES OF URBAN DISORDER

Urban disorders since 1980 have resulted in the destruction and theft of property, and caused injury to those who engage in such events and to the police who seek to contain them.

- In April 1981, Lord Scarman recorded that the disorders which took place in Brixton left the area in a state comparable to an air-raid: 279 police officers and 45 members of the public were injured, and property which included police and other vehicles and 28 buildings were damaged or destoyed by fire. Widespread looting occurred in the shopping area of Brixton.
- In 1985 at the Broadwater Farm Estate in Haringey, London, several buildings and motor vehicles were set on fire, guns were alleged to have been fired at the police, and one police officer, Keith Blakelock, was hacked to death.
- The disorders which occurred in the Manningham area of Bradford in 1995 witnessed attacks on 102 premises and damage which amounted to around £0.5million.

THE REGULATION OF PROTEST AND DISSENT

The state has traditionally viewed extra-parliamentary politics with scepticism. Violence sometimes occurs resulting in disorder, the destruction of property and injury to participants and bystanders. The presence of large numbers on the streets may not simply threaten public order, but may pose a threat to the power of the government, especially if violence occurs which cannot be effectively contained by the police. This may in turn threaten the stability of the state.

THE COST OF DEMONSTRATING

The policing of public order may also impose additional strains on police budgets. For example, the intensity of feelings aroused by motorway construction and the export of live animals resulted in considerable expenditure on policing. The cost of policing protests concerned with the export of live animals between January– April 1995 amounted to £3.5 million at Shoreham and £4.8 million at Brightlingsea. The policing of the Newbury bypass cost Thames Valley Police £12 million by January 1996. The Highways Agency estimated that protests against the construction of the M65 extension in Lancashire amounted to £2.5 million.

THE LAW, PROTEST AND DISSENT

This section looks at how criminal and civil law regulates the ability of citizens to engage in protest and dissent.

COMMON LAW

Most fundamental 'rights' (such as the ability to demonstrate) are rooted in common law. This is not fixed but may be developed or extended by the judiciary, often in response to protest and dissent. This is illustrated by the following example.

Breach of the peace
Breach of the peace is a commonly-used charge against demonstrators and pickets. It is relatively easy to prove and carries a minor penalty which is unlikely to create martyrs to a political cause. But the nature of this offence has been subject to judicial interpretation. An example of this occurred during the miners' dispute of 1984–5. The Kent constabulary had introduced roadblocks which stopped cars in the Dartford Tunnel, in order to prevent striking miners travelling to Nottinghamshire to picket pits which remained working during the strike. This action made a number of assumptions concerning a person's future behaviour, implying that such pickets would act in a disorderly manner when

they reached their destination, and also seemed to be at variance with the freedom of movement usually associated with liberal democracies. However, in 1984 (in the case of *Moss and Others v. McLachlan*), the courts ruled that such police interventions were lawful.

STATUTE LAW

Many governments have created legistation which affects the individual's right to protest or dissent. Three such important Acts are examined below.

THE 1936 PUBLIC ORDER ACT

Legislation which relates to the obstruction of the highway (the 1980 Highways Act), or to obstructing or assaulting a constable in the execution of his or her duties (the 1964 Police Act) has been frequently used against demonstrators since 1945. However, until 1986 the main piece of legislation which related to politically motivated disorder was the 1936 Public Order Act. This was enacted in response to the activities of the British Union of Fascists and their opponents in the 1930s, and imposed prohibitions on the organisation of a paramilitary organisation and the wearing in public of a uniform indicating attachment to a political party. Additionally, the police were empowered to impose conditions on the route taken by processions, and to ban the protests (with the consent of the local authority outside of London) if they anticipated that 'serious' public disorder would arise. Restrictions were further imposed on political expression: section 5 of the Act made it an offence to utter, publish or distribute words or material which were threatening, abusive or insulting. This was subsequently amended by the 1968 and 1976 Race Relations Acts, seeking to apply such actions to racial intolerance.

However, after 1979, extra-parliamentary political activity was often conducted in ways which were not precisely catered for by the 1936 legislation. One major weakness was that the power to ban or re-route events applied only to 'processions', whose key feature was crowd mobility. This law did not apply to static demonstrations which were a feature of the activities of groups opposed to the National Front, and also arose in some industrial disputes, where relatively few pickets were supported by large numbers of demonstrators.

THE 1986 PUBLIC ORDER ACT

Some of the deficiencies in the 1936 Act were remedied in the 1986 Public Order Act. This Act created or redefined a wide range of public order offences (riot, violent disorder, affray, fear or provocation of violence and harassment, alarm or distress). The main purpose of this legislation was to uphold public order by making a wide variety of activities criminal offences. These ranged from organised civil disorder to boisterous behaviour in a public place which comprised of, for example, gangs of youths standing around on street corners whose presence alarmed residents. Approximately 40 criminal charges were introduced to curb these various forms of unruly behaviour.

Some aspects of the new Act specifically related to activities associated with protest and dissent.

- Organisers of demonstrations were required to give advance notice of their intentions to the police, and a new offence of participating in a banned event was introduced.
- The ability of the police to intervene in processions and demonstrations was redefined. If the police believed a procession would result in serious public disorder, they could apply to the relevant local authority to ban it.
- The police were empowered to impose conditions both on processions and other forms of public assemblies, including static demonstrations held in the open air. The criteria used to justify the imposition of conditions were very broad: the police could intervene if they believed an event would cause serious disorder, serious damage to property, serious disruption to the life of a community, or would result in the coercion and intimidation of individuals.

The implementation of the 1986 Public Order Act

The new provisions contained in this legislation provided increased abilities for the police to intervene in a wide range of political activities, including picketing at industrial disputes. The manner in which this Act could be used to stifle protest was illustrated in April 1995 when the assistant chief constable of Essex wrote to every householder in Brightlingsea, advising them to stop demonstrating in connection with live animal exports, and warning them that they faced arrest and imprisonment if they participated in such actions.

THE 1994 CRIMINAL JUSTICE AND PUBLIC ORDER ACT

The 1994 Act was produced against the background of events which were associated with 'disorderly youths'. These included the hippie convoys at Stonehenge, gatherings of New Age Travellers at Castlemorton in 1993, the activities of hunt saboteurs, and the emergence of a rave culture. The resultant 1994 Act sought to uphold social and moral values; it was particularly directed at youth counter cultures and a wide range of organisations involved in various forms of protest and dissent. Part 5 of the 1994 legislation gave the police a wide array of new powers under the heading of 'collective trespass or nuisance on land' which they could utilise against these groups.

KEY PROVISIONS OF THE 1994 CRIMINAL JUSTICE AND PUBLIC ORDER ACT

This legislation sought to regulate a number of activities associated with counter cultural activities:

Raves

The 1990 Entertainments (Increased Penalties) Act had increased the punishment available to deal with rave promoters who failed to obtain public entertainment licenses. The 1994 legislation empowered the police to stop raves if they believed the loudness of the music caused 'serious distress' to the persons living nearby, and authorised action to prevent persons within a five-mile radius travelling to such events.

Trespass

New powers related to trespass applied to common and privately owned land, and further provided for the removal of travellers from places which included scheduled monuments. A new category of 'disruptive trespasser' was introduced: this was defined as a person who trespassed in the open air and stopped a lawful activity taking place by intimidating, obstructing or disrupting that event. This was particularly directed at anti-hunt saboteurs and pro-environment protesters who could be charged with the new offfence of aggravated trespass. Additionally the police could apply to the relevant local authority for an order to prohibit trespassory assemblies for a period of up to four days, and could direct persons 'reasonably believed' to be on the way to such an assembly, not to continue. This was aimed at a wide range of direct action groups and could be used to prevent virtually any demonstration, lobby, picket or vigil.

Further powers were provided to make it easier for squatters to be removed by authorising a displaced or intended occupier (or that person's agent) to use violence to secure entry to premises once an order for possession had been given.

Unauthorised Campers and Gypsies

The 1986 and 1994 measures introduced sanctions against unauthorised campers. The 1994 Act further removed the responsibility placed on local authorities to provide camps for gypsies by repealing Part 2 of the 1968 Caravan Sites Act. The legislation defined 'gypsy' as 'persons of a nomadic habit of life, whatever the race or origin' but excluded persons who were members of organised groups of travelling showpeople or were engaged in travelling circuses.

CRITICISMS OF THE 1986 AND 1994 PUBLIC ORDER LEGISLATION

The 1994 Act, in particular, prompted a wide degree of protest organised by groups such as the Freedom Network and the Coalition Against the Criminal Justice Bill. A number of criticisms were voiced against the legislation passed in 1986 and 1994. As some of the criticisms apply to both Acts, they are dealt with jointly below.

DEMONSTRATIONS AGAINST THE CRIMINAL JUSTICE ACT

Extended police discretion

Both Acts extended the scope of police discretion to regulate protest and dissent. The police alone were empowered to decide whether to impose conditions, and what these conditions should be, on a procession or static demonstration under the 1986 Act. The 1994 Act extended the scope of police discretion by enabling them to be the sole power determining whether activities constituted 'raves', 'trespass' or 'disruptive trespass', and to then take action provided for in the 1994 Act.

Restrictions of protest and dissent

The effect of these Acts was to stifle protest and dissent. This allegation related to matters such as the requirement to give advance notice for processions and demonstrations, and the police's ability to use conditions such as 'disruption to the life of the community' in both Acts in a restrictive manner, either to prevent such activities completely, or to permit them in a form which would reduce their ability to influence public opinion. Additionally, the 1994 Act introduced a wide range of powers which effectively provided the police with the ability to place major restrictions on the freedom of movement, through their ability to define a peaceful, non-obstructive gathering on a highway as a trespassory assembly.

Prejudicial to civil liberties

The civil liberties of those charged with offences under either Act were also adversely affected. In a number of cases the 1986 Act reversed the burden of proof in a criminal trial, so that a person charged with certain offences under the measure was required to prove his or her innocence. The 1994 measure eroded an accused's right to silence, which further undermined the presumption of innocence which had been at the heart of Britain's criminal justice system.

Dubious effectiveness

It is questionable whether social problems can be tackled effectively by the use of the criminal law. The outlawing of collective activities practised by minority groups such as squatters, failed to offer any solution or alternative to the issue which initially encouraged, or forced, them to embark upon such activities or lifestyles.

Groups on the receiving end of such legislation may feel threatened, and this may result in radicalising their activities, thus *increasing* the likelihood of confrontation with the police. Furthermore, attempts to curb the ability to protest or outlaw events such as raves are likely to drive such activities underground. This may increase public disorder. Protest may act as a form of 'safety valve' at which advocates of minority causes can take to the streets and 'let off steam'. Those denied the ability to do this may embark upon actions which are more violent.

THE REGULATION OF TRADE UNION ACTIVITIES

This section briefly examines attempts made since 1979 to regulate trade union activities which, as has been argued above, can be viewed as a form of extra-parliamentary political activity.

CONSERVATIVE REFORMS, 1979 – 1997

Popular unease concerning the unions enabled the Conservative Party to win the 1979 general election, by emphasising the harm done to the nation as the result of industrial disputes which occurred between 1978 and 1979 (dubbed the 'winter of discontent'). The Conservative Party subsequently introduced a range of civil legislation designed to restrict trade union activities. This was an essential aspect of the Conservative objective of controlling inflation, since the power wielded by unions was regarded as a significant contributor to this problem. The way in which these reforms curbed the ability of unions to engage in industrial disputes, is briefly referred to below.

Picketing

The 1980 and 1982 Employment Acts narrowed the definition of a trade dispute to an action between an employer and that organisation's direct workforce. This redefinition was aimed at secondary picketing: the 1980 Act made pickets liable to a range of civil actions if they attended any workplace other than their own, and the 1982 legislation made the pickets' union responsible if it had authorised action of this nature. Further restrictions on secondary actions were contained in the 1990 Employment Act. The 1980 Act was accompanied by a Code of Practice which suggested that six pickets were a sufficient number to state a union's case.

Closed Shop

The term 'closed shop' described agreements reached between employers and a union (or unions) to restrict employment to members of the recognised union (or unions). The 1980 and 1982 Acts included provisions which were designed to weaken this arrangement, the latter Act providing for the payment of compensation to workers who were dismissed for not being union members. The 1988 Employment Act defined industrial action in support of a closed shop arrangement as an unfair (hence illegal) dispute, and the 1990 Employment Act made it unlawful not to employ non-union members.

Trade Union Democracy?

Legislation regulating the internal operations of unions was enacted in the form of the 1984 Trade Union Act and the 1988 Employment Act. The former imposed the requirement of statutory ballots before the commencement of strike action, and the latter specified the rights of individual members to refuse to participate in an industrial dispute, even when it had been sanctioned by a union ballot. Both 1984 and 1988 measures included provisions for the election of trade union executives and general secretaries. The 1992 Trade Union and Labour Relations (Consolidation) Act required a certification officer to keep a list of trade unions and defined their liability in proceedings in tort (ie, a civil wrong or injury which is liable to a claim for damages).

The courts and industrial disputes

The Conservative Party's trade union legislation enabled the courts to intervene in industrial disputes. This intervention would usually take the form of an employer, who was party to a dispute, applying for an injunction to prevent activities which were the subject of legislative restriction, such as secondary picketing. A refusal to abide by an injunction could result in a union being fined or, in extreme cases, having its assets sequestrated (ie, confiscated). Such activities were viewed by many trade unionists as an unwarranted attack on working class political activity, particularly on the ability of one working class person to display solidarity towards another.

Such civil legislation was reinforced by the intervention of the police and the use of the criminal law. This was especially apparent in the 1984–5 miners' dispute. One difficulty with civil law is that its application is often slow even if ultimately effective. The decision of News International to seek an injunction to place restrictions on picketing at their plant in Wapping in 1987 effectively ended the dispute waged by the NGA and SOGAT print unions.

LAW, ORDER AND SOCIAL CONTROL

A Marxist view of the curbs placed on extra-parliamentary political activity between 1979 and 1997 asserted that they arose to curb the dissent of those at the bottom end of the social ladder, who experienced social problems which included unemployment and the dismantling of the welfare state arising from the introduction of a market economy. The criminalisation of protest and dissent through powers given to the police in public order legislation constituted an important aspect of the coercive response of what was termed the 'strong state'. Thus environmental protestors who rejected materialism, the striker whose actions eroded profit margins, or the rebellious underclass which jeopardised social harmony, were examples of groups whose actions were likely to become criminalised by the law, made the subject of special attention by the police, and treated harshly by the courts. This Marxist view rested on the belief that law was a function of the class and power structure of the wider society, and emphasised the manner in which those in positions of power could apply the label of 'criminal' to whole groups of people who posed a threat to the existing social order.

CONCLUSION

Arguments which allege that the reduction of civil and political liberties is an inevitable consequence of capitalism in crisis are associated with Marxist analysis, and challenged from other political perspectives. Conservatives argued that the reforms to trade union practices enhanced the ability of the individual to decide whether to engage in industrial action by reducing the ability of pickets to intimidate; while the attack on the power of trade union bureaucracies meant that decision-making in these bodies was subject to improved accountability. Additionally, the State did not display a consistent bias against those who engaged in protest and dissent after 1979. In the campaign against live animal exports, the Kent Constabulary police took action to remove unroadworthy lorries engaged in the trade from the roads, and government veterinarians also intervened to ascertain the welfare of the animals. The campaign enjoyed success at Brightlingsea when the High Court refused the request of an exporter to place restraining orders on a number of demonstrators, and the police imposed restrictions on the movement of lorries. These actions forced the abandonment of exporting operations.

SUMMARY

After reading this chapter you should be able to evaluate:

- the tactics associated with protest and dissent (namely demonstrations, direct action, industrial disputes and counter cultural protest), and why such activities may result in public disorder
- the factors which may explain the emergence of protest and dissent in liberal democratic political systems
- the causes of, and responses to, public disorder since 1980
- the attempts made after 1979 to regulate protest, especially the 1986 Public Order Act, the 1994 Criminal Justice and Public Order Act, and various reforms to the ability of trade unions to conduct industrial disputes.

STUDY GUIDES

Revision Hints

The study of activities which can result in public disorder can be a discrete area (as in the AEB's option paper *Power and Political Ideas in the UK*), or it may form an aspect of a more general area of study (including the activities of pressure groups and social movements, and the regulation of trade unions). You should therefore be aware of the general context within which various forms of protest, dissent and disorder have occurred since 1979, the positive and negative contributions of such activities to a liberal democratic political system, and the more specific issues concerned with the emergence and regulation of such activities. Look at the circumstances in which protest and dissent occur, the various tactics used, and the factors governing the likelihood of protest and dissent succeeding in attaining its objectives.

Exam Hints

Answering Short Questions on Protest and Dissent

1 Discuss two reasons which explain why the Conservative Party sought to restrict the ability of trade unions to organise industrial disputes between 1979 and 1997.

This question can be answered both from material contained in this section (most notably the view of industrial disputes as a political activity and the concern of Conservative governments to uphold law and order), but also from material taken elsewhere from your course of study (especially the way in which reform of the trade unions was deemed essential to the government's overall economic policy). To answer this question you should identify and fully discuss two explanations for reform, relating this to key provisions of legislation enacted by Conservative governments.

Answering Essay Questions on Protest and Dissent

2 Discuss the role which protest and dissent play in the operations of a liberal democratic system of government.

This question is underlaid by the assumption that the various forms of protest activity discussed in this chapter are political actions (as opposed to mindless acts of violence). To answer this question you should identify perhaps up to three activities referred to in this chapter (such as demonstrations, direct action and urban disorder) and explain how these can be viewed as political activities. You should identify the key features of a liberal democratic political system (which will include the ability of citizens to play a part in the shaping of policy pursued by the government) and suggest how such activities improve the way in which such a system works (eg, by ensuring minority interests are able to be expressed and to force governments to take notice of issues they would otherwise choose to ignore). You should also evaluate the dangers which such activities pose for a liberal democratic political system: rioting or direct action, for example, may be symptomatic of the failures of a liberal democratic political system to cater for the needs of sizeable minorities, and may further threaten the legitimacy of such a system in their eyes.

Practice Questions

1 List *two* ways in which pressure groups using tactics of direct action may undermine parliamentary government.

2 How do you account for the growth of protest and dissent since 1979?

4

THE ORGANISATION AND STRUCTURE OF THE JUDICIAL SYSTEM

Introduction

THIS CHAPTER WILL examine the personnel of the judicial system, the structures and organisations in which they operate, and the role which they perform.

Key Points
This chapter will discuss the following key issues:

- the organisation of the legal profession
- the structure of the civil and criminal courts
- miscarriages of justice
- the role of judges, paying particular attention to the issue of judicial law-making
- the strengths and weaknesses of the system of trial by jury.

THE LEGAL PROFESSION

If a person is prosecuted for a criminal offence, he or she will be required to defend themselves in a court. Here they will seek either to show that they did not commit the crime of which they are accused (by pleading 'not guilty'), or to plead 'guilty' but seek to excuse the action by presenting mitigating circumstances to explain it. Although a person may defend themselves (which is relatively common in a magistrates' courts), it is usual, particularly for a serious charge, to seek the aid of professional experts. In the UK, these are solicitors and barristers.

SOLICITORS

Solicitors deal with the general public who seek legal advice on a range of problems. Solicitors are required to possess either a degree in law, or a non-law degree plus a one year's conversion course, and then to complete a postgraduate Legal Practice Course, followed by undertaking a period of practice (termed 'articles') in a solicitor's office. This training equips them to deal with a very wide range of legal issues, although there is an increasing tendency to specialise. In 1999 there were 75,000 solicitors in Britain with a practising certificate. Solicitors are regulated by the Law Society whose Office for Supervision of Solicitors handles complaints from the general public, overseen by the legal services ombudsman. The perception that self-regulation was proving ineffective resulted in a government amendment to the Access to Justice Bill in March 1999, to provide powers to establish a legal service complaints commissioner.

BARRISTERS

Barristers specialise in one area of the law. They receive their work from solicitors rather than a direct approach from the general public. This may arise either when a solicitor seeks the opinion of a specialist in a case with which he/she is dealing, or when a case goes to court. Traditionally solicitors prepare the paperwork for such cases, and barristers appear in court as advocates to present the case. Today, however, solicitors also have rights to appear in court.

There are far fewer barristers than solicitors. Barristers are required to obtain a degree in law, followed by a one-year postgraduate course regulated by the Bar Council (which serves as the regulating body for this profession). Following successful completion of their professional education, they undertake a period of training (termed 'pupilage') at one of the four Inns of Court.

Queen's Counsel
Senior members of the legal profession may be appointed QCs (Queen's Counsel). This process is known as 'taking silk', because of the silk gowns that QCs wear in court. Historically, only barristers could be QCs, but solicitors are now eligible for appointment. In 1999 there were three solicitor QCs. QCs are viewed as the elite of the legal profession and traditionally, judges were selected from their ranks.

The place of QCs in the modern legal profession is, however, now subject to challenge. Over 100 MPs signed a House of Comons motion in 1999 to call on the Lord Chancellor to abolish this office. The main grounds of concern were that QCs tended to inflate legal costs. Historically, a QC could not appear in court unless accompanied by a junior barrister. Although this practice was theoretically abolished in 1977, it is still widely practiced. Additionally, QCs command high fees when they appear in court where their work is frequently financed out of public funds.

THE MERGER OF THE LEGAL PROFESSIONS?

The rigid distinction between the work of solicitors and barristers was broken down in 1990 when the Courts and Legal Services Act enabled solicitors to appear as advocates in the higher courts. This move was primarily introduced to bring down the costs of legal proceedings. But solicitors were required to undergo a complex procedure to obtain permission to conduct such cases, so that by 1998, only 634 were qualified to do so. In June 1998, the Lord Chancellor, Lord Irvine, sought to enable more solicitors to appear in the higher courts by ending the ability of any one of the four senior judges (the Master of the Rolls, the Lord Chief Justice, the Vice-Chancellor and the President of the Family Division of the High Court) to block solicitors from appearing.

THE SYSTEM OF LEGAL AID

The 1949 Legal Aid and Advice Act gave defendants facing a serious criminal charge the right to proper legal representation in court. Additionally, aid was available to enable citizens to defend or to enforce their rights in civil actions. This measure was an important aspect of securing equality of access to the law for all citizens.

The system of civil and criminal aid was subject to a number of reforms contained in the 1999 Access to Justice legislation. Legal aid for civil and family cases in England and Wales was placed under the superintendence of a Community Legal Service and would be more difficult to obtain. Criminal legal aid became governed by a Criminal Defence Service. The rationale for these reforms was to reduce the cost of legal aid, which was allegedly being bloated by the fees paid to some 'fat cat' lawyers undertaking state-funded criminal cases.

THE COURTS

The Courts are concerned with determining the outcome of both criminal and civil matters. Criminal and civil courts are organised separately. Although this book is not concerned with civil law, a very brief outline of the structure and role of the civil courts is provided, as there is an element of overlap in the jurisdiction of the criminal and civil courts.

THE CRIMINAL COURTS

A criminal trial involves the adjudication of a dispute between a person (or persons) and the State, in which the latter seeks to have the former punished (through means such as fines or imprisonment). There is a division between serious and minor criminal activities which is expressed in terms of:

- *crime which can be tried summarily*: the matter can be dispensed with speedily in a Magistrates' court.
- *crime which must be tried on indictment*: a warrant has to be drawn up. This delays proceedings which are held in a Crown court.

Some crimes can be tried *either* summarily or on indictment (depending on a defendant waiving his or her right to trial by jury).

Trial procedure in England and Wales

A person charged with a criminal offence (termed the 'defendant') will be asked to plead 'guilty' or 'not guilty' to the charge. If the latter plea is entered, it will be necessary for those bringing the charge on behalf of the State (the 'prosecution') to prove their case 'beyond all reasonable doubt'.

In doing this, the British courts utilise the adversarial system of justice in which the defendant and prosecution seek to assert the validity of their own case, by undermining the arguments put forward by their opponents. Many European countries use the inquisitorial system in which the judge supervises the gathering of evidence, and the trial is used as a forum to resolve issues uncovered in this earlier investigation.

THE ORGANISATION OF THE COURTS IN BRITAIN

In Britain the courts are organised in a strict hierarchy.

Magistrates' Courts

These courts deal with the less serious forms of criminal activity (ie, that which can be dealt with summarily), together with a range of criminal matters which can be handled either summarily or on indictment. These courts are staffed either by laypersons (whose appointment relies primarily on local political nomination) or those with training either as barristers or solicitors (who are termed *stipendiary* magistrates). Juries are not used in these courts.

Crown Courts

These were established by the 1971 Crown Courts Act to try the more serious forms of criminal activity (ie, crime which is dealt with on indictment). The use of juries is a feature of the work of these courts.

Court of Appeal

This court hears criminal appeals from Crown Courts and also civil appeals from the County Court and High Court.

House of Lords

This constitutes the final court of appeal for both criminal and civil cases, which derive from decisions initially made by the Court of Appeal in England and Wales, the Court of Appeal in Northern Ireland and non-criminal appeals from

Scotland. Cases are normally heard by a panel of five judges, and the outcome of a case may be determined by a 3:2 majority vote. The small size of this panel gives individual judges considerable influence over particular decisions and contrasts, eg, with the practice of the European Court of Human Rights in Strasbourg, where cases are heard by a larger panel of judges.

LORD HOFFMAN AND GENERAL PINOCHET

The House of Lords is the final court of appeal in both civil and judicial matters. In one case in 1998, however, its decision failed to be binding.

In 1998 the Spanish government applied to Britain to extradite the former Chilean dictator, General Pinochet (who was in Britain at that time), in connection with human rights abuses while he was President of that country between 1973 and 1990. In November, the High Court ruled that this request should be denied, as the General had immunity from arrest and prosecution. However, later that month, a panel of Law Lords voted by the majority of 3:2 to set aside this earlier judgement, thus asserting that Pinochet could be prosecuted.

It was subsequently revealed, however, that one of the five Law Lords (Lord Hoffmann) who had voted to reverse the High Court judgement was the chairman of Amnesty International Charity Limited (the fund-raising arm of the human rights organisation, Amnesty International), which he had failed to disclose. Additionally, his wife worked for that organisation. Pinochet's lawyers thus argued that the General had not received a fair trial in the House of Lords in contravention of the European Convention of Human Rights. Although in many situations a judge's membership of an organisation concerned with human rights would be seen as commendable in a liberal democracy, in this instance it breached the principles that 'justice must not only be done but must be seen to be done', and 'no man is to be a judge in his own cause'.

In December 1998 a different panel comprised of five Law Lords unanimously voted to set aside the first House of Lords ruling and to hear the matter again, before a new panel composed of seven Law Lords. This was the first time that a decision made by the Law Lords had been overturned. However, in March 1999 the second panel of judges voted, by the majority of 6:1, that the General could be extradited to Spain but only for tortures committed in Chile after September 1988, when the Criminal Justice Act made torture an extra-territorial crime under UK law.

The Judicial Committee of the Privy Council

This is composed of sitting and retired Law Lords, including the Lord Chancellor, and Appeal Court Judges. A panel of judges hears cases, and it acts as the final court of appeal in both civil and criminal matters for 16 former British colonies. It exercised this function in October 1998 when it sanctioned (by a vote of 3:2) the execution of a convicted murderer in the Bahamas. One problem with this situation is that cases heard in London fail to appreciate local feelings regarding crimes and their appropriate punishment. Such sentiments led the government of Trinidad and Tobago to suggest in 1998 that its jurisdiction should be ended and replaced by a Caribbean court of Justice.

The Judicial Committee's role has been expanded by the 1998 Scotland Act, the 1998 Northern Ireland Act, and the 1998 Government of Wales Act. The new role of the Judicial Committee to settle devolution issues arising from these measures has effectively transformed this body into a constitutional court.

This structure may be illustrated diagramatically:

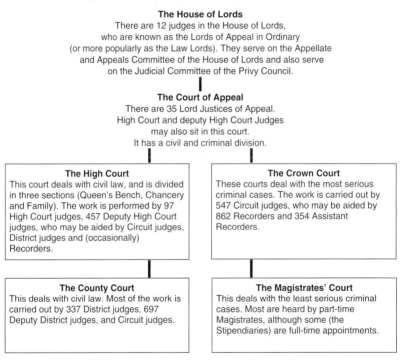

The House of Lords
There are 12 judges in the House of Lords, who are known as the Lords of Appeal in Ordinary (or more popularly as the Law Lords). They serve on the Appellate and Appeals Committee of the House of Lords and also serve on the Judicial Committee of the Privy Council.

The Court of Appeal
There are 35 Lord Justices of Appeal. High Court and deputy High Court Judges may also sit in this court. It has a civil and criminal division.

The High Court
This court deals with civil law, and is divided in three sections (Queen's Bench, Chancery and Family). The work is performed by 97 High Court judges, 457 Deputy High Court judges, who may be aided by Circuit judges, District judges and (occasionally) Recorders.

The Crown Court
These courts deal with the most serious criminal cases. The work is carried out by 547 Circuit judges, who may be aided by 862 Recorders and 354 Assistant Recorders.

The County Court
This deals with civil law. Most of the work is carried out by 337 District judges, 697 Deputy District judges, and Circuit judges.

The Magistrates' Court
This deals with the least serious criminal cases. Most are heard by part-time Magistrates, although some (the Stipendiaries) are full-time appointments.

THE ORGANISATION OF COURTS IN ENGLAND AND WALES

THE SCOTTISH LEGAL SYSTEM

Scotland possesses its own, distinct legal system consisting of District and Sheriff Courts, the Court of Session, and the High Court of Justiciary. Prosecutions are conducted by an official, the Procurator Fiscal, and prosecutors are controlled by the Lord Advocate whose Department is headed by the Crown Agent. Scottish juries (which consist of fifteen persons) have the option of three verdicts – guilty, not guilty or not proven.

Coroners' Courts

The main function of coroners' courts is to hold inquests to determine the circumstances surrounding a death. Juries are used in cases dealing with deaths in prison or police custody, and may be used in other cases at the discretion of the coroner. Witnesses cannot, however, be compelled to answer questions in such courts, and a refusal to answer is not held against them as is normal in criminal trials, where the jury may draw inferences from silence by a witness. The maximum power of the inquest jury is to declare that a death arose from 'unlawful killing'.

THE EUROPEAN COURT OF JUSTICE

This court is staffed by judges and advocates drawn from member countries of the EU. They serve for six years. The main purpose of the court is to ensure that EU law is adhered to within member countries. Disputes between States, between the EU and member States, between individuals and the EU, or between the institutions of the EU are referred to this court. It has the power to declare unlawful any national law which contravenes EU law, and also has the power to fine companies in breach of such legislation. A number of national courts (including those of France and the UK) have upheld the view that European law has precedence over national law. One example of the power wielded by this court over UK domestic law occurred in 1995: the European Court ruled that men in Britain should receive free medical prescriptions at the age of 60 (rather than 65), to bring them into a position of equality with women.

THE EUROPEAN COURT OF HUMAN RIGHTS

In 1950 the Council of Europe (whose membership is wider than that of the EU, with which it should not be confused) drew up the European Convention of Human Rights. This is enforced by the European Commission of Human Rights based in Strasbourg. This body investigates complaints which may be made by States or individuals, and its findings are then considered by the European Court of Human Rights which is also based in Strasbourg. Many European States have accepted its decisions as binding, which has resulted in aggrieved citizens taking their cases to Strasbourg when they do not secure justice in their own countries.

One example as to how this court can affect the UK occurred in 1998 when it ruled (in the case of *Osman v the United Kingdom*) that when the police were aware of a physical threat to a person, they were under a legal obligation to protect that person. This ruling effectively ended the police immunity from legal action in cases alleging negligence, and could be applied to the issue of racial attacks which is discussed in chapter 7.

THE CIVIL COURTS

Civil courts hear disputes between two private parties. The State is not directly involved with the presentation of a case, and the aim of seeking arbitration by the courts is for one party to assert wrongdoing by another. Such may involve the party bringing the case (the 'plaintiff') seeking damages against the defendant. As with criminal courts, civil courts are also graded as follows:

- *Small Claims Courts*: these deal with minor disputes (in which the maximum sum demanded as damages does not exceed £3,000).
- *County Courts*: these deal with a wider range of civil disputes which include actions to secure damages. It also deals with family matters (such as divorce and child custody).
- *The High Court*: this hears the more serious civil cases and is divided into three divisions – the Queen's Bench Division, the Family Division and the Chancery Division.

Appeals from these courts may be heard by the Court of Appeal and ultimately the House of Lords as referred to above.

A person bringing a civil case against another is required to satisfy the judge or judges that the balance of probabilities was that the alleged wrongdoing actually took place. This test is far easier to prove than that used in the criminal courts, and is one explanation as to why those alleging wrongdoing by the police often resort to the civil courts and secure either damages or generous out-of-court settlements.

MISCARRIAGES OF JUSTICE: WRONGFUL CONVICTION

It is an important requirement in liberal democratic States that adequate mechanisms should ensure that mistakes can be speedily rectified. This section examines the manner in which miscarriages of justice resulting in wrongful conviction are dealt with in the UK.

REASONS FOR MISCARRIAGES OF JUSTICE

Miscarriages of justice have traditionally arisen in Britain for one or other of four main reasons:

Inadequate work by defence lawyers

A person may be unfairly convicted because the lawyers defending him or her failed to carry out their job effectively. However, the Court of Appeal has been traditionally reluctant to recognise mistakes by defence lawyers as grounds for appeal, and neither can barristers be sued for negligence in connection with the way they conduct a case in court.

Improper pressure was placed on a defendant by the police to confess to a crime
Such pressure may result in a person confessing to a crime he or she did not commit. This was a particular problem in Northern Ireland when the process of interrogation was utilised to extract confessions related to terrorist crimes. The unique judicial climate in Northern Ireland (provided by the Emergency Provisions Act and the Diplock Courts) underlaid this process, although accusations of unreasonable treatment have been sometimes made in connection with police activity on the mainland. The 1994 Criminal Justice and Public Order Act potentially aggravated this problem (both by eroding the right to silence, and by failing to require corroborating evidence to support confessions).

The fabrication of evidence
The aim of this activity (usually referred to as 'planting' evidence) was to ensure that a watertight case existed against a person(s) strongly suspected by the police of having committed a crime.

Failure by the prosecution to disclose information relevant to the defence
The task of investigating criminal offences is performed by the police. In theory all material relevant to the prosecution's case should be disclosed to the defence who lack the resources to carry out a detailed investigation of their own. The failure to do this may severely prejudice the ability of defence lawyers to defend their client(s). The 1997 Criminal Procedure and Investigation Act, however, potentially worsened this problem by requiring a defendant to make a defence statement, in return for which the prosecution would hand over certain material relating to their case. A police disclosure officer would determine what this consisted of. This reform thus legitimised the non-disclosure of evidence which had formed the basis of some miscarriages of justice.

SOME EXAMPLES OF MISCARRIAGES OF JUSTICE

A number of prominent cases of miscarriages of justice have occurred since 1980. The media played a crucial role in exposing such shortcomings, through programmes such as the BBC's *Rough Justice* and by the efforts of journalists such as Ludovic Kennedy and Paul Foot. Prominent examples of miscarriages of justice have included the following:

- Stefan Kiszko: he was imprisoned for the murder of a schoolgirl in 1975. After spending 16 years in prison he was cleared by the Appeal Court in 1992. Medical evidence proved that it was impossible for him to have committed the crime for which he had been sentenced.
- The 'Bridgewater Four': four men were convicted of the murder of a schoolboy, Carl Bridgewater, in 1978. In 1997 three of them (the fourth defendant having died in 1981) were freed by the Court of Appeal. It was accepted that the case against them was flawed, due to actions which included police fabrication of confessions and failure to disclose evidence to the defence.

DEFENCES AGAINST MISCARRIAGES OF JUSTICE

Two agencies have been established in an attempt to guard against miscarriages of justice.

The Crown Prosecution Service

In England and Wales, the decision whether to prosecute a person for a criminal offence rests with the Crown Prosecution Service, which commenced work in 1986. The operations of this body (which is headed by the Director of Public Prosecutions) are governed by the 1985 Prosecution of Offences Act. The reason for divorcing the investigation of crime from its prosecution was to eliminate bias. It was argued that the close involvement of the police who gathered the evidence with the prosecution of the offence, gave them a vested interest in its successful conclusion. This might be a factor inducing some police officers to apply undue pressure on a suspect to admit guilt. Accordingly, the new system enabled lawyers (who had no previous involvement with a case) to take an objective and dispassionate view of the evidence gathered by the police.

The Criminal Cases Review Commission

Those convicted of an offence by one court may apply to a higher one to seek to have the original verdict overturned. However, the appeals process did not necessarily offer an effective safeguard against miscarriages of justice, especially when persons were charged with offences which posed a threat to the security of the State. The experiences of the 'Birmingham Six' and the 'Guildford Four', who were imprisoned in connection with terrorist offences, indicated the weaknesses of the appeals procedure.

This gave rise to the establishment of a new body, the Criminal Cases Review Commission (CCRC). This body commenced work in April 1997. It consists of 13 members, and was initially chaired by Sir Frederick Crawford. It took over the role previously performed by the Home Office in dealing with alleged miscarriages of justice arising from wrongful convictions. The aim of this body was to restore public confidence in the operations of the criminal justice system, and in particular to provide an effective remedy for innocent people who had been wrongly found guilty by the courts.

THE ROLE AND POWERS OF THE CRIMINAL CASES REVIEW COMMISSION

The ability of the Criminal Cases Review Commission to re-examine a complaint alleging a miscarriage of justice, is governed by two criteria:

- the appeals process must have been completely exhausted
- there must be new evidence (either not available or not disclosed at the original trial or the subsequent appeal).

If these two conditions are met, the Commission has the power to intervene. Initially this will involve a CCRC caseworker questioning applicants and potential witnesses in order to evaluate doubtful cases. Subsequently a re-investigation may be ordered, carried out either by the police or (if a police re-investigation is deemed 'unsuitable') by non-police personnel (such as customs officers, former police officers, lawyers or private investigators). It cannot quash a conviction, but is empowered to refer apparent miscarriages of justice back to the Court of Appeal.

Advantages of the Commission

The Commission possesses a number of advantages over the previous system for dealing with allegations of a misscarriage of justice. These include:

- *transparency*: the operations of this body are far more open than had been the case when such matters were dealt with by a department of the Home Office. A particular feature of its working practices is its willingness to communicate with clients
- *speed*: the Commission tends to work quicker than the Home Office. The first annual report pointed out that in its first year of operation, 1,700 applications alleging wrongful conviction had been referred to it. Reviews of 422 had been completed (around 25 per cent). Seventeen cases (including that of Derek Bentley, executed in 1953) had been referred back to the Court of Appeal, and a further 281 cases were under active consideration.

Problems faced by the CPS and CCRC

Like other agencies in the criminal justice system, the CPS and CCRC function in a political environment. Financial constraints imposed by governments thus have a significant impact on the work performed by both bodies. These have been a factor underlying decisions by the CPS not to prosecute or to downgrade offences, so that they can be heard in magistrates' courts whose operating costs are lower than crown courts. The initial funding arrangements for the CCRC were described by its chairman as 'entirely inadequate' to deal with the volume of work, resulting in undue delay in sentences being reviewed. This situation prompted the House of Commons Home Affairs Committee in 1999 to urge additional funding to deal with the delay in processing cases.

THE JUDICIARY AND LAW-MAKING

The task of judges in the UK is commonly perceived to be concerned with adjudicating in civil and criminal trials. Their role, however, may extend beyond this, to include functions associated with law-making. This section evaluates the manner in which judicial interpretation provides judges with the ability to make law.

INTERPRETATION OF STATUTES

The law-making function of UK judges is facilitated by their need to interpret the law in order to resolve the meaning of words and phrases contained in Acts of Parliament. According to a leading academic legal expert, Michael Zander, there are three basic rules governing this form of statutory interpretation:

1 *the literal rule*: judges rigorously apply the literal meaning of the words contained in a statute regardless of whether the outcome makes sense
2 *the golden rule:* the literal meaning of the words in an Act may be departed from, in order to prevent an absurdity from arising, in which case the judge will look for alternative meanings conveyed by such words
3 *the mischief rule*: a judge departs from the precise language of the statute and instead considers the context within which the Act was passed: this may include considering the 'mischief' which arose in common law which the statute was designed to remedy.

Although the literal rule would normally be followed by a judge in determining the outcome of a case, judicial law-making (which is sometimes referred to as judicial creativity) is facilitated by the application of the golden rule and particularly the mischief rule.

INTERPRETATION OF COMMON LAW

Statutes constitute only one source of English law. There is additionally common law which consists of precedent created either by historic custom, or the earlier decisions of judges which become binding in later, related cases. Judges are especially able to exercise creativity in connection with common law which provides a general warrant for judicial law-making (according to Lord Devlin, a Law Lord between 1961–64). This arises either because the common law is imprecise, or because a judge decides to ignore precedent. Lord Denning (Master of the Rolls, 1962–82) was associated with the latter course of action. He held that his prime purpose as a judge was to secure justice. This implied that when trying a case, a judge was entitled to apply his or her own judgement as to the just outcome, regardless of precedent.

Examples of judicial law-making and the common law:

1 Lord Simmonds proclaimed the existence of the common law offence of 'conspiracy to corrupt public morals' in the Ladies' Directory case (*Shaw v. DPP*) in 1962.
2 More recently in 1998, senior judges, including Lord Chief Justice Bingham, indicated their willingness to develop the common law on breach of confidence into a fully-fledged privacy law, in advance of the enactment of the 1998 Human Rights Act.

A judge's capacity to act as a law-maker is, however, governed by two factors:

- *they are not pro-active*: this means they cannot alter or amend the law unless a case is brought before them
- *the extent to which judges view law-making as a legitimate judicial role*: judges do not have a uniform view on the extent to which they should seek to act as law-makers.

JUDGES AS LAW-MAKERS – THREE CONTRASTING VIEWS

1   Lord Reid (a Law Lord, 1948–74) expressed the minimalist position, or passive approach, to judicial law-making. This held that the courts strictly followed the law, whether established by Parliament or precedents and should not be concerned to bring about changes to it.

2   Other judges have emphasised their desirability to perform law-making through the process of interpretation. Lord Devlin emphasised the importance of the law being shaped according to the prevailing political consensus. Judges should interpret the law in accordance with what public opinion deemed to be acceptable when a decision was required. This view accepted that the political climate within which the judiciary functioned was indispensable in providing legitimacy to its decisions. This was termed 'judicial activism', and involved judges making decisions in line with the prevailing consensus.

3   A final view of judicial creativity extended the concept of judicial activism by arguing that it was acceptable for judges to use the process of judicial interpretation as a mechanism to bring about legal change. This was the 'dynamic' conception of judicial law making and was particularly associated with Lord Denning. An extreme form of this view could be taken to mean that the law was what the judge wanted it to be, rather than what it actually was. Although Lord Denning's judgements were frequently overruled by the House of Lords on appeal, his actions were designed to place pressure on Parliament to bring about a change in the law.

TRIAL BY JURY

There are a number of safeguards designed to ensure that people who come before the courts are given a fair hearing. The decisions of one court can be overturned by a higher court on appeal. Appeals under the 1988 Criminal Justice Act can be made by the Attorney-General, regarding the leniency of a sentence handed out by a judge. A defendant who has been found guilty may also appeal against conviction. Finally, juries may help to ensure that those charged with a serious criminal or civil offence are treated fairly. Their work is discussed below.

THE ROLE OF JURIES

Juries are designed to provide a trial by one's peers (or social equals). They are randomly selected by the jury summoning officer of the court, and their key role is to listen to the evidence which is presented by the defence and prosecution in a trial. They then determine the guilt or innocence of the defendant, based upon an objective consideration of the facts which emerge during the proceedings. In doing this they follow instructions given to them by the trial judge, who further sums up proceedings for them. Initially the universal agreement of all 12 members was required to reach a verdict, but the 1967 Criminal Justice Act permitted majority verdicts of 10:2 in England and Wales.

Betwen 1825 and 1974 there were a number of qualifications needed to serve on a jury, the chief of which was the necessity to be a householder. However, the 1974 Juries Act provided that all persons aged 18–65 whose names were included on the electoral register compiled by local authorities for local and Parliamentary elections, were eligible to serve. This legislation was designed to broaden the social composition of juries, since former qualifications tended to prevent membership drawn from particular key groups in society, especially women. There were, however, certain categories of persons (such as those detained in prisons) who are disqualified from service, and others (such as the clergy) who are ineligible.

There are a number of advantages to the system of trial by jury. These are:

- *they facilitate widespread public involvement in the operations of the criminal justice system*: they are a feature of the criminal justice system in many liberal democratic political systems. Japan, however, is an exception to this
- *they enable popular views of what is right and wrong to influence the operations of the criminal justice system*: this enables the law to be kept in line with public opinion. If a jury feels that the law or the penalties proscribed in it are unreasonable, their ability to pronounce a verdict of 'not guilty' in the face of overwhelming evidence to the contrary may bring about change. However, this action may result in injustices. In America the acquittal in 1992 of Los Angeles police officers who had severely attacked the black American, Rodney King, resulted in riots against the obvious manifesation of racial bias behind such a verdict
- *they are a neutral arbiter standing between the State and its citizens*: juries may safeguard the liberties of the subject, which are of paramount importance in a liberal democratic political system.

PROBLEMS ASSOCIATED WITH THE OPERATIONS OF JURIES

The following section discusses some of the main difficulties associated with the workings of juries in contemporary Britain.

The social representativeness of juries

The system of trial by jury is designed to ensure that a representative cross-section of society give their verdict on an issue which comes before the courts. Juries which are socially representative ensure that the attitudes of one section of society will not dominate judicial decision-making. However, the perception that jurors were 'predominantly male, middle-aged and middle class' has not been totally redressed by the reform introduced in 1974. Women and members of ethnic minority communities remain under-represented, and in 1991 the Commission for Racial Equality concluded that outside urban areas, black defendants were usually likely to face an all-white jury, thus undermining the legitimacy of such a system amongst ethnic minority communities.

There are a number of reasons which explain the jury system's lack of social representativeness. These include non-registration for voting (which although a legal requirement has historically tended to be lower for young people and members of ethnic minority groups). Persons summoned for jury service are able to indicate whether they are available for short or long periods. In 1998 Lord Bingham stated that this resulted in juries for lengthy, complex trials being composed of 'the elderly, the unemployed, the housewife' who constituted 'a rather skewed cross-section of the community'. Additionally, there is a tendency for certain categories of persons to seek exemption when summoned by the jury officer. Professional and self-employed people are least prepared to give up their time or money to serve as jurors, and are thus relatively under-represented on such bodies.

Decision-making by juries

It is difficult to assess accurately how juries reach decisions in Britain. Following attempts by the *New Statesman* to scrutinise the operations of the jury which served in the trial of the former leader of the Liberal party, Jeremy Thorpe, for conspiracy to murder in 1979, the 1981 Contempt of Court Act prevented further journalistic investigation into the workings of juries. Information on this subject has thus been based on alternative methods including experiments involving 'mock juries' or through an examination of the American jury system. The key problems which have been identified in the operations of juries include:

- *the extent to which jury deliberations are dominated by one or two members*: this offsets the benefits of collective decision-making
- *polarisation*: it is possible that decisions may be overly influenced by the process of group dynamics, resulting in verdicts reflecting the views jurors have of each other, rather than being based on the evidence
- *lack of legal training*: this may result in jurors being swayed by factors other than the evidence presented in a trial. In addition to personal prejudices and biases based on class, gender or race, jurors may give undue attention to factors such as body language, the performance of lawyers retained by the

defence and prosecution, or irrational considerations in which a juror's emotions form the basis of a decision

* *jurors may lose track of the evidence*: this is especially likely if a trial takes a long while to complete.

REFORM OF JURIES

Factors such as the time and cost of jury trials, coupled with the belief that innocent people are sometimes acquitted because of the problems, identified above, with jury decision-making, have prompted suggestions that the system of trial by jury should be reformed. There are a number of directions which such reform may take:

Reduce the offences qualifying for trial by jury
This reform would be accomplished by increasing the number of offences which can only be tried in a magistrates' court, thus confining trial by jury to the more serious cases. This reform was contemplated by Michael Howard in 1996 and was subsequently resurrected by the Labour Home Secretary, Jack Straw, in 1998. He envisaged abolishing the right of an accused person to opt for trial by jury in 'either way' cases (that is, where an offence can be tried either summarily or on indictment). These included theft, grievous bodily harm, and some drugs offences, and constituted around 20 per cent of cases currently being heard in crown courts in England and Wales.

Reduce the circumstances under which a person could opt for trial by jury
In 1998 a Home Office Consultation paper suggested that one reform to the system of trial by jury would be to deny a defendant's right to opt for this form of trial if she/he had similar previous convictions to the charges faced. The justification for this would be that such a person no longer had an unblemished record to defend.

TRIAL BY JURY IN ENGLAND AND WALES

In 1997, 104,350 cases were tried before a judge and jury.

Many of the offences which were eligible for a trial by jury were not serious in terms of the nature of the offence or the resulting penalty; they included minor theft. Those accused of relatively small offences may, however, opt for jury trial because they wish to clear their name of the slur cast upon it. Twenty one per cent of jury trials in 1997 (21,783) arose from a defendant opting for this method of trial.

Forty per cent of those pleading not guilty in a crown court were acquitted, compared to 25 per cent in a magistrates' court. This has given rise to a perception that magistrates' courts are more likely to convict, and helps to explain why persons accused of crimes may opt for trial by jury. Research by the Runnymede Trust has indicated that black defendants are especially sceptical of magistrates' courts and prefer to opt for trial by jury.

It is estimated that the average cost of a contested jury trial is £13,500 compared to £2,500 for a case heard in a magistrates' court.

Information taken from Home Office 1998 and the *Guardian*, 29 July 1998.

Change the procedure of jury trials

This reform would enhance the ability of jurors to make objective judgements based on the evidence presented to them. It may include permitting jurors to take notes during the trial, allowing them to question witnesses, and providing them with facilities to see video tapes of the trial to clarify confusing or forgotten issues. Technology may aid, including the use of virtual reality technology, to simplify the task of the jury when it is required to sift through a large number of crime scene photographs.

Streamline the jury system

This would secure a trial by a reduced number of persons. Six are used in many American states and seven were used in Britain during the Second World War. The problems with such a reform include whether this reduced number of persons is adequate to provide either a satisfactory social mix or to permit sufficient robust conversation.

THE REPLACEMENT OF THE SYSTEM OF TRIAL BY JURY

Problems associated with trial by jury have led to suggestions that the system could be replaced, at least in connection with certain types of offences.

In Northern Ireland, trial by jury for what were termed 'scheduled offences' (those associated with politically motivated violence) was abolished in 1973. Trials for such offences henceforth took place before one judge. A major rationale for this reform was the inability to guarantee the impartiality of jurors. However, the accusation of 'case hardening' (that is, the relatively low number of acquittals in contested cases being attributed to the judge having an inbuilt disposition to declare a defendant to be guilty) eroded popular trust in the fairness of this system.

In 1986, the Roskill Commission proposed that complex fraud cases (which frequently result in lengthy trials) should be heard by a tribunal of judges and laypersons with expertise in such matters. The underlying rationale for this reform has been enhanced following the lack of success of the Serious Fraud Office in a number of high profile trials in the 1990s. One (involving the Maxwell brothers) stretched over 131 days and cost the taxpayer an estimated £25 million. At the end of it, all the defendants were acquitted.

SUMMARY

After reading this chapter you should be able to evaluate:

- the organisation of the British legal profession and the rationale for continuing the historic division of responsibilities between barristers and solicitors
- the differentiation between civil and criminal law, and the structure of the court system
- the reason for miscarriages of justice, and the adequacy of safeguards designed to guard against such occurrences
- the debate concerning judges as law-makers
- the strength and weaknesses of the system of trial by jury, and proposals to reform this system.

| STUDY | | GUIDES |

Revision Hints

The material covered in this chapter can be studied in isolation but questions may also be asked in connection with issues raised in Chapter 5. Additionally, the operations of the UK judicial system have been affected by Britain's membership of the European Union, and it is important to be aware of the powers of the European Court of Justice (and also of the European Court of Human Rights). Contemporary developments affecting the role and structure of the courts (such as the involvement of the Judicial Committee of the Privy Council in connection with devolutions issues) should be understood. You should also be able to discuss the work performed by judges (in particular their law-making role), the system of trial by jury, and the role of the new Criminal Cases Review Commission.

Exam Hints

Answering Short Questions on the Judicial System

1 Outline the main responsibilities of the Judicial Committee of the Privy Council.

This question requires an evaluation of the changing, and enhanced, role of this body in contemporary political affairs. You should refer to its role in connection with Britain's former colonies, but devote much attention to examining the nature of its work arising from the three devolution measures enacted in 1998. Specific examples of its activities should be referred to. You could also discuss issues arising from the membership of the Judicial Committee, and perhaps consider whether its role should be performed by a constitutional court (which is an issue discussed in Chapter 5).

Answering Essay Questions on the Judicial System

2   Explain the ability of judges to act as law-makers. In your opinion is this role a desirable one in a liberal democratic system of government?

This question requires an understanding (based on the material above) of how the role of judges extends beyond interpreting the law, and includes the making of it. You should explain this by reference to both the common law and statute law. The component of the question requiring evaluation can, in part, be answered from the material above, in particular the differing views put forward by judges themselves as to whether this is a good or a bad development, and under what circumstances they act in this way. Prominent attention should be devoted to the fact that judges are neither elected nor politically accountable for the decisions which they make, and that their law-making role may involve overturning the policies of a government which may have had a mandate to pursue a course of action to which judges objected. You should additionally refer to material in the following chapter, especially that concerned with the separation of powers which is breached by judicial law-making.

Practice Questions

1   Assess the strengths and weaknesses of trial by jury.
2   Discuss the benefits arising from the establishment of the Criminal Cases Review Commission in 1997.

5

THE CONSTITUTIONAL POSITION
OF THE JUDICIARY

Introduction

THIS CHAPTER ASSESSES the extent to which the judiciary operates independently of the State and the government in the UK, and evaluates attempts by the 1992–97 Conservative government to subject the judiciary to an enhanced measure of political control.

Key Points
This chapter will discuss the following key issues:

- the doctrine of the separation of powers, and the independence of the judiciary
- the appointments procedure for judges and its implications for judicial independence
- the social composition of the judiciary
- the relationship between judges, the State and the government
- the policies pursued by the 1992-1997 Conservative government to subject the judiciary to an enhanced measure of control.

THE JUDICIARY AND THE SEPARATION OF POWERS

The neutrality of the judiciary is theoretically upheld in the doctrine of the separation of powers: the separation of legislative, executive and judicial agencies. This is especially important in defending the citizen from arbitrary actions undertaken by the State. The separation of powers is, however, breached in a number of important ways.

1 *The Lord Chancellor*: this official is a member of both legislative and executive branches of government, and is able to exert considerable influence over the composition and conduct of the judiciary. This issue is explored below in connection with the appointments procedure.

2 *The Treasury*: this department heavily controls the environment within which the judicial system operates.

3 *The Executive Branch takes judicial decisions*: some Acts of Parliament place a minister in a supervisory role (eg, over the actions of a local authority). When exercising this responsibility she/he is required to act judicially and not administratively.

Sentencing decisions involve the executive branch of government in judicial affairs. The determination of release dates for persons serving life sentences is made by the Home Secretary, effectively transforming a judicial decision into a political one. Criticisms have arisen in connection with the use by Home Secretaries of this latter power. In 1997 the House of Lords ruled (in connection with the imposition by the former Home Secretary, Michael Howard, of a 15-year sentence for the two children who had abducted and murdered James Bulger in 1993) that an inflexible minimum period of detention with no allowance for the prospect of rehabilitation was unlawful for a child under the age of 18. Further pressure to reform this situation arose in 1999 when the European Commission of Human Rights determined (in relationship to the trial and sentencing of these same two children) that the Home Secretary was not 'an independent and impartial tribunal'.

THE CASE FOR A CONSTITUTIONAL COURT

The issues raised above suggest that an individual's rights and liberties are insufficiently protected by breaches in the separation of powers affecting the judiciary. This problem is compounded by the ability of the Lord Chancellor, a government minister, to sit in cases which come before the House of Lords, thus denying the defendant a fair trial as guaranteed by the European convention of Human Rights. A similar problem may arise in connection with the work performed by the Judicial Committee of the Privy Council (a body on which the Lord Chancellor can also sit), in connection with devolution issues arising from legislation affecting the government of Scotland, Wales and Northern Ireland which was passed in 1998. These arguments, together with the enhanced role of the judiciary in connection with the implementation of the 1998 Human Rights Act, may justify the establishment of a separate constitutional court whose membership could include judges and laypersons with expertise in such issues.

THE APPOINTMENTS PROCEDURE

The ability of judges to function independently may be affected by the manner in which they are appointed.

MAGISTRATES

Stipendiary magistrates are part of the professsional judiciary and are appointed by the Lord Chancellor. In 1998 there were 91 of these officials, and a further 83 *acting* stipendiary magistrates. Those not legally trained are termed 'lay magistrates' who sit part-time and are not paid for their services. They are appointed by the Lord Chancellor on advice received from 105 Advisory Committees in England and Wales, which are responsible for attracting candidates, sifting through applications, and interviewing potential nominees. These committees are dominated by serving magistrates. Their chairperson is appointed by the Lord Chancellor and is responsible for recruiting other committee members. Local political nomination remains the main source of appointment. In 1996 there were 30,326 active lay magistrates.

JUDGES

The majority of judges in both civil and criminal courts are appointed from the ranks of barristers. On 1 December 1995 only one high court judge, Mr Justice Sachs, was a solicitor. An attempt has been made to broaden the recruitment base for judges so that a greater number of them, in the lower level civil and criminal courts, are solicitors: on 1 December 1995 virtually all (321 out of 322) district judges (who sit full-time in county courts to hear the less important civil and family cases) were solicitors, as were 19 per cent of assistant recorders and 9 per cent of recorders (who sit part-time in crown courts and county courts).

Judges are initially appointed by the Lord Chancellor's Department. In order to become a judge it is first necessary for a candidate to be eligible, as defined in the 1990 Courts and Legal Services Act. This legislation stipulated the number of years' 'right of audience' in the type of court over which the applicant would preside: eg, to serve as a high court judge it is necessary for a lawyer to have rights to appear in that Court for ten years. If eligibility is satisfied, there are further criteria which have to be met. These are embodied in three guiding principles which govern selection:

- *merit*: appointments are made on the basis of merit, regardless of ethnic origin, gender, marital status, sexual orientation, political affiliation, religion or disability. In certain judicial posts, the criteria used to assess merit has been identified
- *'soundings'*: the Lord Chancellor places considerable weight on the views of serving members of the judiciary with knowledge of the performance of a potential candidate for judicial office. These views are gathered by a process of confidential consultation known as 'soundings'. This system enables those already occupying judicial office to secure the appointment of those from a similar background to themselves. One consequence of this has been the tendency for the Law Lords to be selected from the ranks of commercial lawyers, to the detriment of criminal lawyers.
- *proof of competence and suitability*: this requires a candidate for full-time judicial office to serve first on a part-time basis, long enough to establish his or her competence and suitability.

Judges remain in office until they reach the retirement age, which for the majority of judges is 70, as stipulated by the 1993 Judicial Pensions and Retirement Act. The Lord Chancellor may, however, authorise a judge below the level of the High Court bench to remain in office for a period of up to one year, which can be renewed until the judge reaches the age of 75. Once appointed, judges are subject to training and appraisal supervised by the Judicial Studies Board.

How Judges are chosen

Selected applicants are interviewed by a three-member panel, which consists of a senior official of the Lord Chancellor's Judicial Appointments Group, a judicial office holder, and a lay interviewer. The Lord Chancellor makes the final decision to appoint, based on the candidate's application form, the panel's decision, and soundings.

Since September 1994, lower level judicial appointments (which include circuit judges, district judges and assistant recorders) have been advertised, although the Lord Chancellor retained the ability to offer posts to lawyers who had not applied to an advertisement. On 24 February 1998 a further innovation affecting the judicial appointments system occurred with the first advertisement in the *Times* for the post of high court judge. This move was prompted by the fact that the composition of the senior judiciary had changed little in terms of social class, gender or ethnic composition over the last 40 years, resulting in the under-representation of women and members of ethnic minority communities. The advertisement thus advised female and ethnic minority lawyers to 'give this opportunity serious thought'.

The most senior appointments (including Lords of Appeal in Ordinary and Justices of Appeal) are not, however, advertised. Additionally, appointment is not subject to any formal interview or selection panel. Instead, appointments are made by invitation from existing lower level judges whom the Lord Chancellor (following soundings from other senior judges) estimates to be outstanding. These senior judges are then recommended for appointment to the Queen by the Prime Minister.

PROBLEMS WITH THE PRESENT SYSTEM OF JUDICIAL APPOINTMENTS

There are a number of problems associated with the present method of choosing judges, especially the most senior members of the judiciary. These are discussed below:

Political interference
One major difficulty with the appointments process is that it gives the executive branch of government a considerable influence over the composition of the judicial branch. Although the Home Affairs Committee argued in 1996 that they had received 'absolutely no evidence that the present Lord Chancellor has used his powers of patronage regarding judicial appointment to favour those who shared the ideology of the government', they were more sceptical of the role played by the Prime Minister's involvement in the appointment of the most senior judges.

The problem with political influence over the composition of the judiciary is that it performs the process of judicial review, one aspect of which involves adjudicating on the legality of actions undertaken by the executive branch of government. This issue is discussed later in this chapter.

Not socially representative
Despite recent attempts to open up the process of appointment, the perception remains of judges as elitist. This is especially so regarding education: in 1999 Labour research pointed out that 80 per cent of senior judges were educated at public schools and 86 per cent had attended Oxbridge. Appointments made by the Labour government since 1997 have worsened rather than challenged this situation. Additionally, relatively few women and members of ethnic minority groups are appointed to judicial office. This gives rise to a perception that the individual or institutionalised prejudices of judges may result in women and ethnic minorities being unfairly treated by the courts.

THE SOCIAL COMPOSITION OF THE JUDICIARY

'Judges come from a remarkably similar background, male, white, public school and Oxbridge, which has changed little in the past 50 years. There are no women among the Law Lords, only one among the 35 Appeal Court Judges, and seven among the 97 High Court Judges. Ethnic minorities are completely absent from the higher judiciary. There are no black full-time judges at any level, and only four (mainly Asian) ethnic minority Circuit Judges out of 558'.

Clare Dyer, *Guardian*, 5 August 1998

Such social unrepresentiveness is not, however, deemed to be a significant problem by senior members of the legal profession. In 1990 the then Lord Chancellor, Lord Mackay, asserted that it was 'not a function of the judiciary to be representative of the people as a whole'. In 1997 the Labour Lord Chancellor, Lord Irvine, stated that while he was keen to increase the number of women judges, promotions would continue to be made on merit without the use of positive discrimination measures. He also rejected positive discrimination to increase the number of black judges, although he announced measures to develop more effective appraisal and assessment mechanisms to help individuals improve their performances as judges, and the introduction of a scheme to allow prospective applicants to 'shadow' judges.

REFORMS TO THE APPOINTMENT PROCESS

A number of reforms might be suggested to remedy the problems outlined above. These are discussed below.

A Judicial Appointments Commission

One solution to the problems of political bias and social unrepresentativeness would be to transfer the appointment of judges from the executive branch of government to an independent Judicial Appointments Commission. Members could be drawn from a number of interested parties, including serving members of the judiciary, legal academics, representatives from the two branches of the legal profession and lay persons. This proposal (which would additionally result in the abolition of the system of soundings) was rejected by the Home Affairs Select Committee in 1996. This reform might also detract from the principle of ministerial accountability for decisions relating to appointment.

The Hearings System

This procedure enables an assessment to be made of the suitability of the candidate's views and opinions for the public office they wish to hold. It is used in a number of liberal democratic states, such as America, in connection with a wide range of appointments to senior government office. This procedure has not been commonly used in Britain, although the House of Commons Treasury Select Committee did adopt such a process in 1997 for appointees to the Bank of England's Monetary Policy Committee. It would compel potential judges to disclose their opinions and beliefs on a wide range of issues which are relevant to their work.

One further justification for extending this procedure to senior judicial appointments is that their role was broadened following the incorporation of the European Convention of Human Rights into British law in the 1998 Human Rights Act. This innovation may justify an examination of the views and attitudes of senior judges in the area of human rights and civil liberties, since the Law Lords would act as the final UK court of appeal in matters which include privacy and the relationship between the State and the individual.

THE JUDICIARY AND FREEMASONRY

A hearings system requires judges to defend their opinions prior to appointment, thus providing a defence against personal bias and prejudice. This issue was addressed by the Labour government in 1998 in connection with freemasonry. The perception that those who operated in the criminal justice system (including magistrates, police officers, lawyers employed by the CPS, prison staff and probation officers) and who belonged to this secret society would discriminate in favour of fellow masons prompted the Home Secretary, Jack Straw, to request that the Freemasons' governing body, the United Grand Lodge, disclose the names of judges who were masons. Their failure to do so resulted in the Lord Chancellor's department sending a questionnaire to all magistrates and judges on this matter in July 1998. He informed the House of Commons Home Affairs Select Committee on 10 November 1998 that responses to the questionnaire sent to magistrates revealed that 13.6 per cent of male magistrates who responded to the questionnaire (females not being eligible to join) had disclosed their membership of the masons, and a further 5.4 per cent had failed to reply to this question. Of the full- and part-time judges 4.9 per cent had disclosed their membership, and 64 of the respondents failed to answer the question.

THE JUDICIARY AND THE STATE

An important issue concerning the relationship between the State and its citizens concerns the impartiality of the judiciary. Although the separation of powers is designed to ensure that judges function in an impartial manner, the extent to which this is possible is subject to debate. A very broad division of opinion separates what might be labelled 'liberal' and 'Marxist' opinion, concerning the neutrality of the State, law and hence the work of judges.

Liberal analysis suggests that the State is neutral. That is, it has no interests to defend, and advances the views held by the majority of its citizens. Crime is viewed as an act which breaches society's rules, which are supported by the majority of its citizens. It follows from this that the law seeks to embody the common perception of right and wrong, and that in enforcing the law, judges merely reinforce such popular attitudes.

Marxist analysis, however, questions these liberal assumptions. Marxists believe that the State is not impartial but, rather, seeks to defend and advance the interests of those who hold economic power within society. The law, therefore, is not neutral but seeks to perpetuate the unequal property relationships which exist within society. Thus judges, when enforcing the law, are not acting in the interests of all citizens but perpetuating the inequalities which underpin it. The Marxist view that the operations of the State and the content of the law exist to serve the interests of the ruling class, highlights the problem of securing popular consent to both. They assert this is achieved through the ideological apparatus of the State which propagates the myths of the neutrality of the law and the impartiality of judges.

TWO VIEWS CONCERNING JUDICIAL IMPARTIALITY

The Marxist assertion that judges are a key component of a state which serves the interests of the economically powerful in society, has practical consequences for the manner in which they allege judges function. John Griffiths, a neo-Marxist, put forward this view when he declared that judges 'operate as an essential part of the democratic machinery of administration' who are concerned 'to preserve and protect the existing order'. This statement implies that those people whose actions pose fundamental challenges to the State or the values which underpin it, cannot receive impartial treatment by judges. Judges decide what is in the 'public interest'.

Griffiths asserted that judges have acquired a 'strikingly homogeneous collection of attitudes, beliefs and principles' as to what 'public interest' consists of. This is based on their common experiences derived from education, training and pursuit of the profession as a barrister. The perception that all judges adhered to the view that the public interest embraced 'the interests of the State (including its moral welfare) … the preservation of law and order; and … the promotion of certain political views normally associated with the Conservative party', led him to conclude that 'it is demonstrable that on every major social issue which has gone before the courts during the last 30 years – concerning industrial relations, political protest, race relations, government secrecy, police powers, moral behaviour – the judges have supported the conventional, established and settled interests'. A further example of a circumstance in which a definition of the term 'public interest' was required concerns cases when the public's 'right to know' is challenged by the State's requirement of 'official secrecy'.

However, such an assertion has been challenged by the 'pluralist' position. This disputes the Marxist argument that the actions of judges are characterised by what a uniformity of approach dictates. Roshier and Teff cite the occurrence of clashes between the Court of Appeal and the House of Lords as evidence that there is no single conception of public interest, and state that while most judges are conservative, there are elements of 'independence and variety' to be found amongst them: although a 'conservative, formalist approach to interpretation is a distinctive feature of the judicial tradition, many judges display a bluff, no-nonsense pragmatism and a few are conscious social reformers'.

PLURALISM: THE IRAQGATE TRIALS

The absence of a consistent direction pursued by judicial decisions can be illustrated by two trials related to 'Iraqgate' (involving the sale of arms to Iraq by British companies). A common feature of these trials was the attempt by the government to utilise Public Immunity Certificates to withhold material from the defence, on the grounds that this would prejudice national security. The trial judge had the ability to support this supression of evidence or overrule it.

- In the first case, involving the firm Ordtec in 1992, the trial judge agreed with the government's actions. Following plea bargaining, two persons were given suspended sentences, and one was fined in connection with trying to export a shell fuse assembly line to Iraq.

- In the second case, involving Matrix-Churchill, the judge overruled the government, and the trial quickly collapsed in 1992.

PAUL HENDERSON OF MATRIX CHURCHILL WITH A COPY OF THE SCOTT REPORT, ON THE ARMS-TO IRAQ INQUIRY, 1996

JUDGES AND GOVERNMENT POLICY

The defence of *State* interests needs to be differentiated from the defence of *government* interests. While it is open to debate as to whether the judiciary display a relatively consistent line in connection with the State, their actions are less constant when a matter which is referred to them for adjudication has significance for the *policy* of the government, but not the *interests* of the State.

JUDICIAL REVIEW

The doctrine of the separation of powers implies the independence of the judiciary from the executive branch of government, which is an especially important consideration in connection with the task of judicial review. One aspect of this work involves the courts examining the actions of the executive, to ensure that they are legal.

JUDICIAL REVIEW – SOME EXAMPLES

Traditionally the doctrine of parliamentary sovereignty meant that the courts were restrictive in their approach to judicial review, but this stance altered in the 1980s and especially in the 1990s when judges regularly utilised this process to overturn actions undertaken by governments. Examples include:

- *1995*: the Court of Appeal delayed the process of rail privatisation by a decision which hinged on the interpretation of 'minimum standards'
- *1996*: the High Court set aside the decision of the then Home Secretary, Michael Howard, to expel the Saudi dissident, Professor Mohammed al-Mas'ari, to Dominica
- *1998*: the Court of Appeal ruled that the Labour Home Secretary, Jack Straw, had acted illegally in refusing an asylum application by a Nigerian woman and ordering her deportation on the same day, thus denying her the ability to exercise her right of appeal
- *1998*: the High Court ruled that the Secretary of State for the Environment, Transport and the Regions, John Prescott, had acted unlawfully when he agreed to a plan to construct 113 new homes on a greenfield site in Peacehaven, East Sussex. The Judge ruled that the Minister and a public planning inquiry inspector had failed to properly consider the concerns of the local authority.

Although the willingness of the judiciary to act independently of the executive branch of government, in connection with the process of judicial review, upheld the spirit of the separation of powers, such decisions projected the judiciary forcefully into the political arena, and could be viewed by governments as an attack on their ability to govern.

THE CONTROL AND ACCOUNTABILITY OF THE JUDICIARY

The doctrine of the separation of powers requires the judiciary to have a considerable degree of independence. This is necessary to ensure that they treat those who come before the courts in an impartial manner, and do not operate as functionaries (ie, agents) of the governing political party. The need to avoid judges being manipulated by the executive branch of government, resulted in the relative absence of sanctions related to their professional conduct. The 1992–97 Conservative government altered this situation by imposing central control over sentencing issues.

SENTENCING

Judges traditionally possessed a wide degree of freedom in determining the sentences of those convicted in their courts. In some matters (such as the mandatory sentence of life imprisonment for murder) they had no room for manoeuvre, but in others they could exercise considerable choice. The discretion exercised by the judiciary posed a number of problems. These included:

Inconsistent sentencing
Those found guilty of similar offences could receive widely different punishments depending, it appeared, on the whim of the judge. This conflicted with the principle of equal treatment under the law.

Excessive leniency
Conservative ministers perceived that the criminal justice system in general, and judges in particular, were often treating offenders too leniently, which undermined the government's image as being 'tough' on criminals. This view was endorsed by the 1996 British Crime Survey, in which four out of five respondents asserted (albeit on the basis of grossly inaccurate perceptions) that judges were too lenient in their sentencing policies. An early intervention was the 1988 Criminal Justice Act, which gave the Attorney-General the power to appeal against excessively lenient sentences. This perception of judicial leniency encouraged attempts by the government to impose a greater degree of ministerial control over the sentencing policies of the courts, which is discussed below.

CONSERVATIVE REFORMS TO SENTENCING

In 1996, a government White Paper, *Protecting the Public: The Government's Strategy on Crime in England and Wales*, put forward wide-reaching interventions in sentencing policy.

- Offenders convicted for a second time of a violent or sex offence would receive automatic life sentences unless there were 'genuinely exceptional circumstances' which the court would be required to justify. Judicial discretion concerning life sentences was limited to determining whether these were appropriate for offences including arson, kidnapping and false imprisonment.
- Offenders aged 18 or over who were convicted of drug-trafficking offences involving class A drugs with two or more previous convictions for similar offences, would receive a mandatory sentence of seven years. This approach was popularly referred to as 'two strikes and you're out.'

- Offenders aged 18 or over who were convicted of domestic burglary, and who had three or more convictions for similar offences, would receive a mandatory sentence of three years. This approach was popularly referred to as 'three strikes and you're out'.

The 1996 White Paper was subjected to a number of criticisms:

Constitutional objections

Ministers were accused of interfering in the operations of the judiciary. Lord Donaldson, a senior judge, argued that the transfer of sentencing powers from the judiciary to the executive branch of government posed a threat to the freedom of the individual citizen; Lord Hailsham, a former Lord Chancellor, declared that mandatory sentences imposed upon the independence of the judiciary.

Injustice

The government's approach was based on the principle of deterrence through punishment and harsh sentences. However, this approach went beyond any concept of 'just deserts', since punishment took into account the offender's previous criminal record. This could mean that repeat offenders might receive a harsher sentence than that merited by the specific crime they had committed. It was alleged that injustice could result from this approach. Judges dispense justice, rather than exact revenge for criminal behaviour. In assessing a just sentence, the judge needs to take all circumstances which have been revealed during the trial into account. This would no longer be possible when sentences were pre-determined. Additionally, such proposals might result in minor offenders receiving overly-severe sentences. This would increase the costs of a trial, since it was likely that defendants, knowing the sentence in advance, would be more likely to plead not guilty.

Encourage violent crime

Judges also feared that the Home Secretary's proposals might increase the murder rate, since a rapist would have no incentive not to kill his victim if the mandatory sentence for both crimes would be of the same length.

THE 1997 CRIME (SENTENCES) ACT

The government's White Paper was subject to a hostile reception in the House of Lords on 23 May 1996. In response to such criticisms, some amendments were incorporated into the subsequent 1997 Crime (Sentences) Act. These included a 20 per cent discount on the new mandatory minimum sentences for a timely plea of guilty. Changes were also proposed which enabled judges to exercise an additional degree of discretion in sentencing.

HONESTY IN SENTENCING: TIME SERVED IN PRISON

The 1990 White Paper, *Crime, Justice and Protecting the Public*, and the resultant 1991 Criminal Justice Act, introduced significant changes in the practices connected with releasing prisoners before they had served the full sentence dispensed by a court. These provisions sought to reduce the amount of discretion exercised by the prison authorities, so that the courts would possess a greater ability to determine the actual sentence served. The 1996 white paper sought to achieve this philosophy of 'honesty in sentencing'. In line with these suggestions, the 1997 Crime (Sentences) Act introduced key reforms to sentencing policy. These were:

- All custodial sentences were scaled down to two-thirds of what would have been the case before the Act was passed.
- For offenders sentenced to over two months but less than three years', imprisonment could earn early release at the rate of twelve days for each two months of their sentence.
- Prisoners sentenced to over three years' imprisonment were not eligible to earn early release days, but would be eligible for release by the Secretary of State in accordance with a recommendation of the Parole Board after five-sixths of the sentence had been served.
- Prisoners would not be released on license, but those sentenced to 12 months or more would be subject to a 'release supervision order', which would usually be equivalent to one-quarter of the length of the sentence.

THE NEW PUBLIC MANAGEMENT AND THE COURTS

The courts and crown prosecution service, like the police service, became subject to the new public management. The philosophy of the *Citizen's Charter* was specifically applied to the courts by the publication of the *Court's Charter* in 1992, which became effective in 1993. This document set out what citizens could expect when they came into contact with the courts, and what could be done if something went wrong. In particular, it set out standards of service and performance which those coming to court as jurors, witnesses or defendants should receive. A separate *Victim's Charter* was also published which explained the rights and expectations of people who were the victims of crime. Annual reports by the three departments most directly concerned with the courts (namely, the Lord Chancellor's Department, the Crown Prosecution Service, and the Home Office) were also published.

THE 1997 LABOUR GOVERNMENT AND THE JUDICIARY

The Labour government inherited the Conservative party's sentencing reforms, which were slowly introduced. In June 1998 an armed robber with previous convictions for rape became the first offender to be given a life sentence under the 'two strikes and you're out' policy of the 1997 Act. The trial judge informed him that before the new law was implemented he would have received a sentence of seven years. The policy of 'two strikes and you're out' was initiated in December 1997; the Home Secretary deciding that previous convictions would not count in the application of this rule. This meant it was unlikely that any burglar would receive the mandatory sentence until mid-2001.

At the 1992 general election, the Labour Party had proposed the establishment of a Sentencing Council, whose role would be to produce guidelines on a range of cases, thereby ensuring a greater level of consistency between the courts on sentencing policy. In office, the government introduced a system whereby the magistrate or trial judge provides full details concerning a sentence. This information entails announcing the minimum time to be served with parole, the minimum time without parole, the maximum term possible, and the earliest release date. The victim of the crime would be informed in writing of the sentence and the earliest possible release date.

SUMMARY

After reading this chapter you should be able to evaluate:

- the extent to which the doctrine of the separations of powers is upheld in connection with the judiciary
- current issues concerned with the social composition of judiciary (including the under-representation of women and ethnic minority communities), and reforms to the appointments procedure
- the relationship between judges and the State, and judges and the government, and the importance of the process of judicial review
- the motives which prompted Conservative governments to increase their control over the operations of the judiciary, and the problems associated with this approach.

STUDY 🅔 GUIDES

Revision Hints

The starting point for answering questions related to material in this section is the separation of powers. You should fully understand this concept and be able to discuss the manner in which it applies, and does not apply, to the constitutional position of the judiciary. The operations of the appointments process is a good example of the way in which this principle is breached. The social composition of the judiciary is an important issue, whose elite nature may be linked to a more general discussion of the power of the 'establishment' in Britain. You should further be able to analyse the constitutional position of the judiciary, distinguishing between its autonomy from the State, and also from the government. The process of judicial review should be understood, supported by a number of examples. You should be familiar with the way in which the Conservative government sought to enhance central control over the operations of the judiciary, particularly with regard to sentencing policy, and also with the criticisms made of this approach. This theme might be combined with the attempts by Conservative governments to secure an enhanced measure of control over the police service: this issue is discussed in Chapter 6.

The material in this chapter is closely related to the issues in Chapter 4, concerning the structure and law-making role of the judiciary.

Exam Hints

Answering short questions on the judiciary

1 Outline two examples of the way in which the judiciary is subject to the control of the executive branch of government, and the dangers which arise from this.

To answer this question, you should first cite examples of executive control over the judiciary: you might include the appointments procedure, reforms to sentencing introduced in 1997, or attempts to influence the performance of the judical system through the *Court's Charter*. Your discussion of the dangers associated with such control should start with a discussion of the separation of powers, explaining why the independence of the judiciary is important in a liberal democratic political system, and then move on to considering some specific problems arising from the examples you have cited. You might argue, for example, that the executive branch of government has too much influence over the appointments procedure, and that this could be used to undermine the judiciary's ability to act independently of the government.

Answering essay questions on the judiciary

2 To what extent did the relationship between politicians and the judiciary alter during the 1990s?

Initially, you should introduce the concept that the separation of powers should protect the judiciary from political control. You should then consider two ways in which this concept was breached during the 1990s. Examples might include the reasons for passing the 1997 Crime (Sentences) Act, together with an assessment of the problems raised by this approach; or it could involve a detailed discussion of the manner in which the process of judicial review was used in this period, and the difficulties caused by the more aggressive use of this role, for Britain's liberal democratic political system.

Practice Questions

1 How effective is the separation of powers in enabling the judiciary to function as an independent branch of government?
2 Why are judges socially unrepresentative, and what measures might be put forward as a solution to this situation?

6

THE GOVERNANCE, STRUCTURE AND ORGANISATION OF THE POLICE

Introduction

THE THEME OF this chapter is the transformation of policing from agencies controlled by local government into a more centralised service in which central government performs a dominant role. There are two aspects to this discussion – changes to the governance (ie, the control and accountability) of policing, and reforms to its structure and organisation. This chapter analyses the background to the changes which have occurred, the manner in which they have been affected, and the problems which have arisen as a result of them.

Key Points
The chapter will discuss the following issues:

- key legislation: the 1964 Police Act, the 1984 Police and Criminal Evidence Act, the 1994 Police and Magistrates' Courts Act, and the 1997 Police Act
- the rationale for changes made to the governance of the police after 1964
- the impact of Conservative reforms on the performance culture of the police service after 1979
- changes affecting the structure and organisation of policing.

MECHANISMS OF CONTROL AND ACCOUNTABILITY FOR THE POLICE SERVICE

Policing in Britain (with the exception of London) used to be controlled by local government. Separate police forces were formed, rather than one national police service. The almost exclusive control exerted by local people over policing was, however, affected by two developments which originated in the nineteenth century. These were:

- the involvement of central government in police work. Key developments were the 1856 County and Borough Police Act (introduced a government grant towards the cost of local police forces, subject to a government inspection declaring that it was conducted efficiently), and the 1919 Police Act (resulted in a number of activities related to policing, such as pay and conditions of service, becoming determined centrally by the Home Office)
- the desire by chief constables to exert influence over some of the activities performed by the forces which they headed. This gave rise to demands by chief constables for autonomy (ie, the ability to determine police policies themselves rather than being told what to do by local government). The term 'constabulary independence' is used to describe this situation.

THE 1964 POLICE ACT

By the middle of the twentieth century, the control of policing was shared by local government, central government and chief constables. However, the separation of responsibilities was unclear and a more precise division between these three bodies was needed. The 1964 Police Act sought to achieve this objective. Its main provisions are outlined below.

LOCAL GOVERNMENT

The 1964 Police Act ended direct control exercised by local government over policing outside of London. Local control would now be exerted by a police authority, which in most areas was initially a committee of the local council. Two-thirds of the membership of this body were councillors, and the remaining one-third were magistrates. The role of the police committee was to maintain an 'adequate and efficient police force for their area', and they were provided with a specific range of functions associated with this duty. These included:

- powers of appointment and dismissal of senior officers
- the determination of the establishment (ie, the number of police officers employed) of the force
- the maintenance of premises and equipment.

Additionally, police authorities acted as disciplinary bodies for the chief, deputy and assistant chief constables, and could require the chief constable to submit a report in writing related to the policing of the area.

THE CHIEF CONSTABLE

The 1964 Police Act placed each force under the 'direction and control' of its chief officer, whose prime responsibility was to enforce the law and maintain the Queen's peace. The legislation gave the chief constable a number of day-to-day functions in relation to the administration of the force (which included the appointment and dismissal of officers up to the rank of chief superintendent, and investigating all complaints made against any junior officers).

CENTRAL GOVERNMENT

The Home Secretary exercised a prerogative power to maintain law and order. The 1964 Police Act gave this Minister a range of strategic and tactical responsibilities designed to promote the overall efficiency of the police service. These included powers:

- to pay or withhold the government grant
- to require police authorities to retire their chief offficer
- to make regulations connected with the 'government, administration and conditions of service of police forces'
- to appoint inspectors of constabulary, and instruct them to carry out duties to further increase police efficiency
- to exercise control over the standard of equipment used by police forces
- to supply and maintain a number of services available to the police service generally.

The Home Secretary could require a chief constable to submit a report on the policing of an area, and to order a local enquiry on any police matter. The enquiries by Lord Scarman into the 1981 Brixton disorders was an example of the use of this power.

AN ASSESSMENT OF THE 1964 POLICE ACT

The 1964 Police Act gave rise to a number of subsequent problems.

Control of police responsibilities
The division of responsibilities was put forward in vague language. This led to the existence of grey areas, which could become a battleground as to who had the final say in determining a particular activity. This issue formed the background of notable disputes between chief constables and their police authorities in Greater Manchester and Merseyside in the early 1980s.

The tripartite system of accountability
The mechanism of police accountability used to be straightforward. Outside London, policing was controlled by local government, to whom the police were accountable for their actions. The division of control provided for in the 1964

Police Act was termed 'tripartite'. In practice, however, it made for an unwieldy and ineffective system of accountability.

THE TRIPARTITE SYSTEM OF POLICE GOVERNANCE

Under this system, accountability consisted of a complex system of checks and balances. Actions undertaken by the Home Office, chief constables or police authorities were subject to scrutiny by one or both of the other bodies involved in policing. There were two problems with such a system. First, it made for ineffective accountability, as the actions initiated by one body could be cancelled out by the intervention of another. For example:

• A police committee could require a chief constable to produce a report on police activities, however, the chief constable could appeal to the Home Office to override this request.
• A police committee could appoint and dismiss its chief constable, but the Home Office could set aside its decision on such matters.

Second, the sanctions which one body could use to influence the actions of another were inadequate. For example, the Home Office could withold the government's grant if it deemed a police force to be operating inefficiently. But the practical impossibility of bankrupting a police force meant that this penalty could never be applied in the post-war period, even in situations where it might have been justified.

There were other deficiencies in the 1964 Act. Police authorities were not directly accountable either to a local authority, or to local voters. Although the Home Office was accountable to Parliament for the exercise of its functions related to policing, the system was imperfect. This inadequacy was only partially remedied with the introduction of a new Select Committee on Home Affairs in 1979, which has periodically conducted investigations into aspects of police work.

POLICE ACCOUNTABILITY IN THE 1980S

THE DEMAND FOR POLICE ACCOUNTABILITY TO
LOCAL COMMUNITIES

The 1980s witnessed disputes in some areas between police authorities and chief constables. The key issue was an attempt to make chief constables more accountable for their actions to local opinion, especially when formulating priorities concerning police activities. These disputes were most intense in Greater Manchester and Merseyside. The demand for enhanced police accountability to the local public was based upon four separate factors:

Public involvement in policy-making

Public participation in local government policy-making had been officially promoted since the late 1960s; eg the Town and Country Planning Act of 1968, and the subsequent publication of the Skeffington report, People and Planning, in 1969. The objective of increased public involvement in a wide area of local government services was subsequently pursued during the 1970s. Policing was inevitably affected by this climate, as it was organisationally attached to local government.

The politicisation of policing

Perceptions of the politicisation of policing arose after 1979. As Chapter 3 argues, those on the left of the political spectrum viewed the police as a coercive instrument which advanced Conservative monetarist economic policies by countering the dissent which arose from people who became unemployed and unemployable. Police actions became directed against industrial disputes, protest and inner-city disturbances, and this led to policing becoming controversial: the term 'Maggie's boot boys' suggested that the role of the police was to promote government policy, rather than serve the needs of all members of society. This argument supported the demand for enhanced local accountability during the miners' dispute, 1984–85, when it became obvious that local police authorities had no power to prevent their police officers being sent to preserve the peace in parts of the country where coal mines remained working during the national strike.

The urban left of the Labour Party

Some local authorities fell under the political domination of the Labour Party's 'urban left' following Labour's defeat in the 1979 general election. These sought to construct a socialist society 'from the bottom up', using local government as the launch pad for this ideology. This approach required local government to extend its control over a wide range of policy areas, including the police. However, chief constables were unwilling to yield major changes in the relationship between chief constables and police authorities, and responded to the demand by turning to the Home Office for support. The Home Secretary could override police authorities when they clashed with their chief officer over matters such as the provision of equipment. This procedure initially strengthened chief constables in their dealings with police authorities, but in the long term, such reliance promoted the Home Office as the pre eminent power in police affairs.

Corruption and abuse of power

Allegations of corruption and abuse of power provided further support for improved mechanisms of police accountability to the general public. Issues such as the death of Jimmy Kelly in Merseyside police custody fuelled perceptions that abuse of power sometimes occurred because of the lack of effective supervision over the actions of police officers. As Chapter 3 argues, a particular problem in the 1970s and early 1980s was the searching of persons and vehicles. Police powers to undertake these activities were derived either from local legislation or the 'sus' provisions of the 1824 Vagrancy Act (which was repealed in 1981 and replaced by the Criminal Attempts Act). It was alleged that some officers used powers of this nature in a random fashion, based not upon the likelihood of a person being engaged in an illegal activity, but upon criteria which included colour of skin, style of dress or simply being in what was regarded as a 'high crime' neighbourhood. Concern was further expressed about the aggressive way in which policing was often delivered. Units such as the Metropolitan Police's Special Patrol Group were singled out for particular criticism.

Accusations of corrupt behaviour were also made. Between 1978 and 1982, Operation Countryman investigated alleged corruption by members of the City of London and Metropolitan Police Force. Forty-one officers were reported to the Director of Public Prosecutions, and four were subsequently prosecuted.

MAIN PROVISIONS OF THE 1984 POLICE AND CRIMINAL EVIDENCE ACT

The protest and dissent which took place in a number of urban areas in 1981, ensured that there would have to be an official response to the demands made for improved mechanisms of police accountability to local populations. This was initially delivered through Lord Scarman's report, many of whose recommendations were included in the 1984 Police and Criminal Evidence Act.

The 1984 legislation was particularly motivated by the desire to satisfy demands for improved accountability. It introduced reforms to enhance the extent to which the police operated with the consent of the general public. Such reforms were anticipated to result in improved standards of police behaviour, creating better relationships between police and public, especially in urban areas. This situation would therefore render unnecessary any fundamental changes to the structure of police accountability. Reforms to methods of policing (especially community policing) were also kick-started by Scarman's report.

The main provisions of the 1984 Act were:

Safeguards to the exercise of police powers

One solution to the problems arising from the use of stop and search powers would have been to remove them entirely from the armoury of police resources. The police asserted, however, that these powers were essential to the effective discharge of their duties. Thus the government's response in the 1984 legislation was to retain them, but govern their use by the introduction of safeguards.

- Stop and search could only be conducted if an officer had reasonable suspicion that it would produce evidence of criminal activity.

- The officer making the search was required to give the suspect his or her name, the location of the police station to which he or she was attached, the object of the search and the grounds for undertaking it.
- A person who had been stopped and searched was entitled to a copy of the record of the search.

Safeguards were also introduced to cover:

- the detention, treatment and questioning of a person by the police
- identification procedures
- (more recently) the tape recording of interviews.

The Act also imposed additional restraints on police actions, which included stipulating the length of time a suspect could be detained at a police station, and providing for supervision of a suspect by the new post of 'custody officer'. All Codes were revised in 1991, when a suspect's right to legal advice was emphasised.

The main problem with safeguards was that they were embodied in codes of practice. The breach by an officer of any aspect of these codes was not a criminal offence, although it might be the subject of a disciplinary charge. This meant that the influence which the codes exerted over the actions of police officers on the streets was partly dependent on their willingness to abide by them; this was reinforced by the stance which judges adopted towards such breaches in cases which subsequently came to court.

The Police Complaints Procedure

The ability to make individual officers answer for their actions is an important element of police accountability. The 1964 Police Act had introduced a common system for handling complaints by members of the general public against police officers. The 1976 Police Act considerably developed the procedure by establishing a Police Complaints Board, whose role was to consider complaints alleging that an officer had breached police disciplinary regulations. Under the provisions of the 1976 Act, complaints from members of the general public were monitored by the force's deputy chief constable. The complaint was then investigated either by officers from that force's Complaints and Discipline Department, or by those drawn from another force. If this led the deputy chief constable to believe that a criminal offence may have been committed, a file was sent to the Director of Public Prosecutions, who would then decide whether or not to prosecute that officer.

However, if the deputy chief constable felt that the investigation had revealed no evidence of a criminal offence, or if the Director of Public Prosecutions decided not to initiate a prosecution, the deputy chief constable could prefer a disciplinary charge against the officer complained against. It was at this stage that the Police Complaints Board became involved: it could recommend that disciplinary charges should be brought against the officer, and ultimately could insist on it. Alternatively, it could call for further investigations into the matter.

A number of other criticisms were made against the operations of the 1976 Act. A major problem was that the public were sceptical of a procedure in which complaints against the police were investigated by the police themselves, even if this involved officers from other forces (invariably the case when serious complaints were made). Aggrieved citizens were often loathe to make an official complaint, and people who alleged police wrongdoing began to resort to the civil courts for a remedy.

The 1984 Police and Criminal Evidence Act sought to respond to some of the criticisms of the police complaints machinery. Its main features were:

- *the abolition of the Police Complaints Board*: this was replaced by a Police Complaints Authority (PCA), whose responsibility was extended to cover complaints of both a criminal and disciplinary nature
- *an enhanced role for the PCA*: all serious complaints made against police officers (including death, serious injury, actual bodily harm, corruption and serious arrestable offences) were automatically notified to this body, which was empowered to *supervise* the investigation of them. Supervision involved approving the appointment of an investigating officer, imposing requirements on the conduct of an investigation, and receiving a report from the investigating officer
- *the ability to complain directly to the PCA*: members of the public could complain directly to the PCA, rather than having to enter a complaint at a police station, which had been the previous practice. This process was used in 2,000 instances in 1997
- *powers*: the PCA possessed the power to overrule a chief constable and instruct this officer to send a report to the Director of Public Prosecutions, or to recommend (and ultimately, insist) that disciplinary charges should be brought.

These amendments provided a half-way-house situation between the independent examination of complaints and the internal investigation of them.

Liaison machinery

Lord Scarman's enquiry addressed the issue of police–public relationships. He suggested a compromise to reconcile the claims of the police for professional autonomy, with a desire by many members of the public for greater involvement in police work. Section 106 of the 1984 legislation required police authorities outside London to make arrangements to secure the views of the public on the policing of their area by establishing consultative committees. Consultation involved no change in the power relationship between police and the public: the police merely agreed to listen to what members of the public had to say, but were not required to act upon it.

RESULTS OF REFORMS TO COMPLAINTS AGAINST THE POLICE

Police corruption
Reforms to the police complaints procedure failed to solve the problem of corrupt behaviour by a small minority of police officers. In 1989, the West Midlands Serious Crimes Squad was disbanded and an investigation was initiated into its activities. Although this led to a number of convicted criminals being freed by the Court of Appeal, no officer was convicted of an offence. Alleged police malpractice at Stoke Newington police station in Hackney, London, in the early 1990s resulted in the Metropolitan police paying £1 million in damages and costs, and two officers being jailed. In 1997 the Chief Commissioner Sir Paul Condon, informed the House of Commons Home Affairs Select Committee that there were around 250 corrupt officers in his force.

Ineffective complaints system
Reforms made to the police complaints system in the 1984 legislation failed to transform it into an ineffective device for punishing officers guilty of serious disciplinary offences. In 1997/98, 18,354 complaints were made, but few were upheld, mainly due to insufficient evidence.

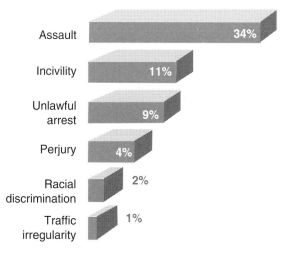

Assault	34%
Incivility	11%
Unlawful arrest	9%
Perjury	4%
Racial discrimination	2%
Traffic irregularity	1%

REASONS WHY PEOPLE MAKE COMPLAINTS AGAINST THE POLICE.

Duncan Campbell, the *Guardian* 26 June 1988.

Key problems with the complaints system include:

- *No link with civil actions against the police*: in the *Observer* on 14 February 1999, Graham Smith estimated that Scotland Yard paid out around £3 million in 1998 to settle or compensate civil claims made against them, and the Greater Manchester Police paid in excess of £2 million. The police often settle these claims out of court, usually refusing to accept any liability or even apologise for the incident. Details of such awards and the circumstances which prompted payment are not always made public, and officers involved in such actions may escape any sanction.

- *The vast majority of complaints against the police are thrown out*: reasons for this include the absence of adequate evidence to support a complaint, the right to silence in connection with an allegation, and the very high standard of proof ('beyond all reasonable doubt') required to substantiate it.

- *Officers guilty of disciplinary offences frequently escape sanctions*: they may do this by retiring (thereby keeping full pension rights), taking extended sick leave, resigning or agreeing to an 'admonishment' (ie, a reprimand). This issue was raised in connection with the officers involved in the investigation of the death of Stephen Lawrence in 1993, and is discussed in Chapter 7.

- *Double jeopardy*: officers acquitted in criminal trial cannot subsequently face a disciplinary charge in connection with the same issue.

- *Lack of independence*: the police remain responsible for investigating complaints. This situation may create an impression that police officers investigating other colleagues will not always pursue a complaint with the vigour which they would deploy in other criminal matters. Additionally, members of the PCA are appointed and dismissed by the Home Secretary, who may in some cases give guidance to them.

The ineffectiveness of the system led to criticisms from the European Commission of Human Rights in 1998 in connection with a complaint by Michael Govell, whose home had been illegally bugged by the police. The Commission found that his right to privacy had been violated, and the complaints system had denied him redress. The Home Secretary, Jack Straw pledged to introduce reforms which included lowering the burden of proof against officers (so that in April 1999, this test was reduced to the civil one of 'the balance of probabilities'), removing their 'right of silence', and introducing a six-week 'fast track' system to deal with serious allegations. The Home Office also commissioned a study to examine whether an independent system was needed and could be afforded.

THE CHANGED CLIMATE FOR POLICE ACCOUNTABILITY

The pressure for enhanced mechanisms of police accountability was not sustained during the 1980s. The abolition of the metropolitan counties in 1986 resulted in the police authorities for such areas becoming joint boards, composed of magistrates and representatives from the constituent councils. This development reduced the demand to improve mechanisms for local police accountability since police authorities in metropolitan areas were no longer associated with any single local authority, and could no longer claim a mandate for their demands.

Additionally, changes to the balance of power within the Labour Party resulted in the loss of influence by the left, who had been most associated with demands for police accountability. This tended to tone down the party's official criticisms of police performance and the power of chief constables to determine policy. Although the Party continued to advocate a greater role for police authorities in police affairs during the 1992 general election campaign, the rationale presented for this reform was directed at the growing influence exerted by the Home Office over police affairs, and not the excessive power of chief constables.

CENTRAL CONTROL OF THE POLICE SERVICE

Control over the police service was traditionally enforced by:

- *legislation*: this imposed responsibilities on the police service. However, as it is impossible for the police to enforce every single piece of legislation, priorities indicating the most important tasks to be performed were drawn up. Such prioratisation was largely the responsibility of chief constables
- *circulars*: Home Office circulars were a major source of influence over the operations of the police service after 1919. These are not legally binding, but were usually treated as if they had such authority
- *inspection*: the process of inspection was introduced into the police service in 1856. Inspections served to alert ministers to problems in particular parts of the country, and also provided them with a mechanism to influence the working practices of police forces
- *informal controls*: statements by senior politicians often guided the actions of the police service in a political direction. For example, a statement by the then Prime Minister, John Major in 1994, that street beggars were offensive and that the law should be enforced against them, was a strong inducement for the police to act vigorously against such persons
- *the Treasury*: the cost of the police service (the great bulk of which was derived from central government) was a major item of public spending. Constraints imposed by the government have major implications for its operations. As is discussed below, the application of the Financial Management Initiative after 1983 had a fundamental impact on the way in which policing was delivered.

Changes introduced into the police service after 1979 were directed at its working practices (or performance culture) and governance. Both served to increase the degree of control over the police service and are discussed in greater detail below.

REFORMS TO THE WORKING PRACTICES OF THE POLICE

The following section discusses key initiatives introduced after 1979 to enhance the efficiency of the police service.

Policing by objectives

Initially the police service did not suffer from the scale of public spending cuts inflicted on other public services after 1979. However, the perception that increased spending on the police was not reducing crime and disorder levels, prompted a change of direction by the government. The principles of value for money and effective use of resources which were embodied in the 1982 Financial Management Initiative were applied to the police service by circular 114/1983 (*Manpower, Effectiveness and Efficiency in the Police Service*), and developed by subsequent circulars. Police forces responded by adopting the system of 'policing by objectives', which required them to specify their objectives and the means through which they would be implemented. The 1983 circular was viewed as a major step towards centralisation, by increasing pressure on individual forces, to produce similar results to other forces.

The Audit Commission

Conservative policy to achieve efficiency and value for money allowed a variety of central agencies to intervene in police affairs. The role of the Audit Commission (established by the 1982 Local Government Finance Act) had a major bearing, especially when it was empowered by the 1992 Local Government Act to establish performance indicators for the police. This enabled it to publish annual league tables, which contained comparative information on issues such as the level of crime and the detection rates in each of England and Wales's 43 police forces. Many of its reports (such as the investigation into police patrol activities, *Streetwise*, published in 1996) exerted a major influence on the management of police forces, and the way in which they performed their tasks.

New public management

The police service has become subject to 'new public management'. This approach was based upon the *Citizens' Charter* which was launched in 1991, designed to improve the choice, quality, value for money and accountability of public services.

Performance culture is a particular concern of new public management, which has sought to transform the public's perception of the police by market forces, rather than through political structures of accountability. This requires transforming the general public from citizens into consumers, who become better informed of police affairs and more able to insist upon high standards of efficiency. Police authorities subsequently played a key role in this process by preparing local policing plans (a development discussed in the following section). Many individual police forces also used customer surveys to determine levels of public satisfaction with specific aspects of service delivery.

PRIVATISATION OF POLICING

Privatisation constituted an important aspect of new public management. The performance of policing functions by bodies other than the regular police is not a new development. It emerged in the nineteenth century and accelerated after 1945, when factors such as the traditional dislike of British workers for bank accounts required payrolls to be collected from banks and taken to firms and factories by commercial companies. However, further progress was made in this direction as the consequence of policies pursued by Conservative and Labour governments after 1979. The growth of this sector of policing can be attributed to two developments which are discussed below.

THE GROWTH OF THE COMMERCIAL POLICING SECTOR

The precise size of this sector is unknown, but it dwarfs the numbers employed as regular police officers. In 1994, research by the Policy Studies Institute estimated that there were around 100,000 persons employed as security guards, patrolmen, night-watchmen, gate-keepers and related security-type workers, and the government's 1999 White Paper on the regulation of the private security industry quoted a turnover figure of £2.1 billion for the industry in 1992. The size of the commercial policing sector was one factor which prompted the Labour government in 1999 to suggest establishing a self-financing Private Security Industry Authority. This would issue licenses to individuals wishing to form companies or to seek employment in a wide range of activities performed by private security guards. Penalties would be introduced for people who either worked in this capacity without a license or who ran a company without a license.

The privatisation policies of the Conservative governments, 1979–97

Consumerism pursued by Conservative governments in the 1990s sought to subject the police service to the discipline of the market. However, the attainment of this objective was handicapped by the absence of competition in most areas of police work, which would enable the aggrieved citizen to go elsewhere for police services. The desire to provide effective forms of competition was an objective of privatisation policies to policing, a key aspect of which was 'load shedding' (whereby services were relinquished to commercial or voluntary service providers).

The attempt to decide which activities could be relinquished by the police was handed to a Home Office review team in 1993, charged with differentiating between core and ancillary functions. A series of recommendations were presented, which supported a principle of privatisation whereby non-core functions could either be off-loaded onto commercial or voluntary sector providers, or made subject to compulsory competitive tendering (introduced in the 1988 Local Government Act).

However, the growth of the commercial policing sector in the 1980s was not totally at the expense of the functions previously performed by the regular police. Many activities performed by the commercial sector were significantly or totally underpinned by civil law, and were not carried out by regular police forces.

The crime and disorder policies of the Labour government since 1997

One aspect of the 1998 crime and disorder legislation was the introduction of crime audits, enabling local people to express their concerns regarding crime and disorder. This approach would almost inevitably formalise pressure for more police patrols to respond to problems such as hooliganism, stray dogs, and litter, at a time when restraints on police budgets made it impossible for police forces to devote increased resources to such work. However, the shifting of routine patrol work to private bodies and local authorities provided a potential solution to this dilemma. In 1999 the Metropolitan police announced the launch of a pilot scheme in four areas of London, whereby routine patrol work would be shifted from the police service to other agencies including uniformed council staff and other private bodies. Two of these schemes would be licensed by the police, and the other two by local government. A nationwide warden patrol scheme for council and housing estates which would recruit unemployed people was announced by the Home Secretary in 1999.

Best Value

This initiative was introduced into local government by the Labour government in 1998, and later became a statutory obligation imposed on police authorities. It sought to promote economy, efficiency and quality of service provision, and the approach was underpinned by setting targets and measuring performance against them. This replaced compulsory competitive tendering, but was not underlaid by any suggestion that services should be passed either permanently or temporarily to the private sector. This new approach placed the onus on local service providers to demonstrate to a process of independent audit that they were providing best value.

THE REFORM OF POLICE GOVERNANCE: THE 1994 POLICE AND MAGISTRATES' COURTS ACT

Many of the developments discussed above tended to increase the role of central government in police affairs. The implementation of the 1983 circular, for example, provided the inspectorate with a key role, namely to report on police efficiency, and to identify and disseminate good practice. Additionally, an attempt was made to subject the police service to an enhanced degree of central control, particularly in connection with the determination of police priorities.

The need for the police service to provide good value for money was put forward as the underlying rationale for the government's proposals which were embodied in the 1994 Police and Magistrates' Courts Act. This provided for:

- *national objectives*: the Home Secretary would set national objectives for the police accompanied by performance indicators to assess their attainment, thus effectively enabling ministers to move the police into areas which suited their own political purposes. The practical impact of this was that henceforth ministers, and not chief constables, would determine police priorities
- *cash limits*: cash limited budgets would be introduced, giving the government total control over expenditure. Its contribution towards the budget for each force was based on a Standard Spending Assessment; this was derived from the 'crime index' based upon five key policing activities
- *amalgamation of police forces*: simplified procedures would be introduced for amalgamating forces. It was argued that the existence of 43 separate forces in England and Wales did not make the most effective use of resources available for policing.

Home Office control was underpinned by changes to the composition of police authorities, whose key role was to draw up an annual local policing plan to contain a statement of national and local objectives, performance indicators and finances available. Under the new arrangements, a police authority would normally consist of 17 members – nine councillors, three magistrates, and five independent members appointed by the police authority from a short list prepared by the Home Secretary.

HOME OFFICE NATIONAL OBJECTIVES

In 1995–6 these consisted of the following:

- to maintain, and if possible increase, the number of detections of violent crimes
- to increase the number of detections of domestic burglaries
- to target and prevent crimes which were a particular local problem, including drug-related criminality, in partnership with other public and local agencies
- to provide high visibility policing, in order to reassure the public
- to respond promptly to emergency calls from the public.

There are two contrary views regarding the impact of the 1994 Act on the subsequent development of the police service.

Enhanced central control

While the Act retained the tripartite system of police governance which had been developed in the 1964 Police Act, the balance between these three partners was substantially altered. This opinion asserts that chief officers were reduced in status, subjected to enhanced central control, and relegated to providing services determined by police authorities in their local policing plan. The latter were themselves subject to increased central direction exercised by the Home Office.

However, the view that the 1994 legislation had a negative effect on the power of police authorities in favour of central control, depends on the balance which is struck in local policing plans between national and local objectives. This is likely to change under the Labour government. The partnership proposals in the 1998 crime and disorder legislation envisaged increased local involvement in the formulation of crime prevention strategies. This could serve to enhance the importance attached to local issues.

Increased managerial responsibilities for senior police officers
Alternatively, the 1994 Act gave chief officers full management responsibility for all police personnel, and the ability to direct and control local policing within the context of the local policing plan and the Home Office's cash limited budget. The chief constable will almost inevitably play a major role in drawing up the local policing plan for the local police authority, and his or her role may be further enhanced if costed policing plans are introduced, since the information on which these would be based will be provided by the police force. The increased tendency for local commanders to be given control of their own budgets within the framework of the local policing plan, will also serve to enhance the power of these officers. This trend was further aided by the 1998 Crime and Disorder Act which strengthened the relationship between divisional commanders and chief executives of local authorities.

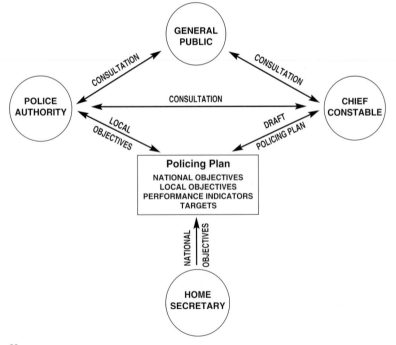

HOW A POLICING PLAN IS PREPARED

Adapted from Greater Manchester Policing Plan 1996–7

THE STRUCTURE AND ORGANISATION OF POLICING

The above section argues that policing in Britain has been transformed, from agencies controlled by and accountable to local government, to a service in which central government plays an increasingly significant role. Other changes have also taken place which affect its structure and organisation, creating a more centralised service. These changes are discussed briefly below.

THE CHANGING NATURE OF CRIME

Crime has significantly contributed towards the changing nature of policing. Its decentralised organisation was appropriate when crime was a predominantly local affair, carried out by individual criminals. However, in postwar Britain, crime became more organised, controlled by criminal masterminds who recruited teams for a particular enterprise, often utilising violence to achieve their aims. This resulted in spectacular crimes involving vast sums of money, such as the 'great train robbery' in 1963. The enhanced mobility of criminals was matched by police reorganisation which initially (during the 1960s) took the form of regional crime squads, operating across police force boundaries. Further developments connected with the national and international organisation of crime resulted in the following changes.

The development of national organisation
During the 1970s, a number of national squads were formed to gather intelligence on activities which included the drugs trade, illegal immigration and football hooliganism. These units were brought together in 1992 under the organisational umbrella of the National Criminal Intelligence Service (NCIS). This was controlled by the Home Office, and was designed to coordinate the activities of a number of agencies concerned with such crimes. Additional functions were subsequently added to the responsibilities of NCIS. This body had no executive arm, although its regional organisation matched that of the regional crime squads, which were themselves subject to a loose form of national coordination based in London.

The 1997 Police Act placed the NCIS on a statutory footing. It also established a new national operational unit, the National Crime Squad, which was especially concerned with serious crime of relevance to more than one police force in England and Wales. Under this legislation the Home Office relinquished its control of the NCIS; two 'service authorities', reflecting the tripartite composition of police authorities (composed of independent members appointed by the Home Secretary, representatives of the Association of Chief Police Officers (ACPO), police authorities and the Home Office) were established. This measure also established a Criminal Records Agency to facilitate criminal background checking on an estimated eight million job applicants each year. The purpose of this reform was to enable employers to demand a criminal conviction certificate from potential employees.

The New Role of MI5

The end of the Cold War resulted in MI5 acquiring new functions. In 1992 it was assigned the lead role in countering terrorism on mainland Britain. The IRA ceasefire necessitated the development of further areas of responsibility. Accordingly, the 1996 Security Services Act allocated MI5 the responsiblity for dealing with 'serious crime' in addition to its existing functions. This was a contentious issue. A particular problem was that MI5 was not accountable in the same way that police forces were when performing this task. It also posed the possibility of demarcation disputes arising between the police and MI5.

The police service was concerned about such developments, fearing that MI5 would assume the lead role in serious crime and become a *de facto* national police organisation, the British equivalent of the American FBI. Such concerns arose as only MI5 had specific legal power to enter a person's premises and plant a bugging device for surveillance purposes. Accordingly, ACPO and the NCIS urged police powers in connection with bugging to be placed on the same legal footing as MI5's. This innovation was introduced in the 1997 Police Act, which provided the police with powers to 'bug and burgle', using methods such as hidden cameras and listening devices to prevent or detect serious crime. Civil liberties were to be protected by a code of practice to govern surveillance operations, and by appointing a Surveillance Commissioner who would consider complaints and make an annual report to Parliament.

THE EUROPEAN DIMENSION TO POLICING

Britain's membership of the European Community had implications for the workings of the criminal justice system, and the organisation of British domestic and international policing. The need to standardise policing practices across Europe (especially to combat crimes including terrorism and drug-trafficking) resulted in a number of initiatives, including the 1985 Schengen Treaty and the formation of the TREVI group (foreign ministers of the EU). The end of the Cold War and the opening of the previously sealed borders of central and Eastern Europe aggravated these problems, and created new ones, especially in connection with refugees fleeing the war in Yugoslavia. The 1991 Maastricht Treaty provided for the development of a European-wide police force, EUROPOL whose objectives were defined in the 1995 EUROPOL convention as 'preventing and combating terrorism, unlawful forms of drug-trafficking and other serious forms of international crime where there are factual indications that an organised structure is involved'.

THE SCHENGEN TREATY

The Schengen Treaty operates outside the framework of the Maastricht Treaty, and its philosophy is also compatible with the establishment of a European-wide police force. There are a number of aspects to this agreement, including:

- the establishment of a database (initially known as the Schengen Information System) with descriptions of people and objects wanted or missing in each Schengen country
- cooperation over drugs-related crime (especially designed to limit drug smuggling)
- closer harmony of police operations across national frontiers (which includes the ability of German police officers to pursue suspects for up to 10 km inside Holland)
- simpler extradition rules between member countries.

A further aspect of Schengen was the abolition of frontier controls. The United Kingdom was, however, sceptical of this development, believing that while open EU frontiers made sense for law-abiding citizens, criminals might also benefit. For this reason, therefore, the UK remained outside of Schengen, a course of action affirmed by Tony Blair at the Amsterdam summit in 1997.

The role of the National Crime Squad envisaged cooperation with police forces across Europe, a particular target being the multi-national career criminal. Bilateral cooperation between the British and French police has also occurred, for example, in connection with policing arrangements for the 1998 World Cup football tournament.

POLICE-GENERATED CHANGES

The police service has also been responsible for changes which have promoted centralisation and standardisation. Two of these are discussed below.

The growth of technology

The increased use of technology has contributed towards the centralisation of policing. The ability of police officers anywhere in the country to access certain basic information such as criminal names, wanted or missing persons, stolen firearms and registered vehicles was enhanced by the introduction of the Police National Computer (PNC) in 1969. The PNC has subsequently been developed by Phoenix, which provides the police with instant access to records of arrests, convictions and cautions. Following the launch of the National Strategy for Police Information Systems in 1994, all police forces should report information in a standardised fashion. This application enables all forces to record crime data in a standard format. The ability of the police to respond to major incidents involving criminal activity carried out in several parts of the country, and thus necessitating cooperation by different police forces, was enhanced by the Home Office Large Major Enquiry System (HOLMES).

The policing of public disorder

The policing of public disorder has tended to transform British policing into a more standardised and centralised form.

- *Mutual aid*: this involves one police force being able to summon assistance from others when faced with a serious public order situation. The 1964 Police Act effectively made it obligatory to provide such aid in this circumstance. The decision to apply for mutual aid used to be in the hands of a chief constable faced with disorder. Since 1972, however, this matter has been determined centrally; in that year the ACPO established a mechanism which was initially known as the National Reporting Centre (now termed the Mutual Aid Coordination Centre). This body operated from New Scotland Yard, was operationally under the control of ACPO's president, and became activated when an event arose with major implications for public disorder. Its role was to coordinate the deployment of police officers throughout the country to the area affected by disorder. This arrangement was utilised in the miners' dispute of 1984–5, and gave rise to allegations of the development of a centralised system of policing.
- *Police public order training*: standardisation has also occurred in connection with police public order training. A key development was the publication in 1983 of ACPO's *Public Order Manual of Tactical Operations and Related Matters*. Each force was issued with a detailed analysis of the stages of a riot and the police responses appropriate to them. A total of 238 tactics and manoeuvres were set out in its 30 sections arranged in order of escalating force, from normal policing up to the use of plastic bullets, CS gas and live firearms. The publication of the *Public Order Manual* was accompanied by the formation of an ACPO body, the Public Order Forward Planning Group, to review all new developments and emerging tactics.

Further developments affecting standardisation arose following the miners' dispute. All forces were required to train a number of Police Support Units (which consist of uniformed police officers who receive a limited degree of public order training on a regular basis) to common standards, one advantage being that an officer from one force could then command PSUs drawn from other forces. These centralising initiatives were especially detrimental to the role exerted by police authorities over policing.

POLICING IN SCOTLAND AND NORTHERN IRELAND

The structure of policing in Scotland and Northern Ireland differs from that in England and Wales.

In Scotland, policing was reorganised under the provisions of the 1973 Local Government (Scotland) Act, reducing the 22 police forces to eight, whose boundaries largely coincided with the regions then used for Scottish local government purposes. These forces are superintended by police boards whose composition is different from those in England and Wales, comprising only of councillors drawn either from the local council or (in the case of forces operating in more than one local authority area) from a special joint board of councillors from the constituent local authorities. The Scottish Secretary was historically responsible for the operations of the Scottish Inspectorate of Constabulary.

The Northern Irish policing system was based on the system used throughout Ireland when the entire country was part of the UK. Since 1921 there has been one police force, the Royal Ulster Constabulary (RUC) for the six counties comprising Ulster. It was initially controlled by the devolved government at Stormont, but since 1970 has been supervised by a Police Authority for Northern Ireland (PANI). This led to a tripartite system of police governance which was similar to that in England and Wales, save that the powers of the Secretary of State for Northern Ireland were greater than the Home Secretary's powers in relation to police forces (other than the Metropolitan police). The close alliance which nationalists perceive existed between the RUC and the Protestant community has generated pressures for fundamental reform of policing. This issue was initially embraced by the Conservative government in 1994, and efforts have been intensified since the 1998 Good Friday peace agreement. This matter is currently being considered by an investigation chaired by Chris Patten.

SUMMARY

After reading this chapter you should be able to evaluate:

- the operation of the tripartite system of police governance introduced by the 1964 Police Act
- the reasons why demands for enhanced local control over police affairs were made after 1979
- the workings of the 1984 Police and Criminal Evidence Act, particularly with regard to the police complaints system
- the rationale for attempts by the Conservative Party to increase the extent of central direction over the police service, culminating in the 1994 Police and Magistrates' Courts Act
- the reason for changes to the structure and organisation of policing and the problems associated with such developments.

STUDY 🄯 GUIDES

Revision Hints

The material in this chapter primarily addresses the transformation of policing in Britain from a localised service to one which has been increasingly centralised and controlled by central government. You should be aware of the main legislation affecting the governance of the police, and also appreciate additional factors which have affected the structure and organisation of contemporary policing; be able to discuss why such changes have occurred and the criticisms that have been made of it.

A further issue which is relevant to this topic concerns the development of police powers: this includes the use of controversial ones such as the old 'sus' law and the manner in which the 1984 Police and Criminal Evidence Act sought to regulate their usage. This topic could also include refer to material contained in Chapters 2 and 3, regarding the political importance of crime (which might necessitate increased police powers), and the development of police powers in connection with public disorder.

Questions may also be asked concerning the behaviour and/or practices of the police: this includes issues referred to in this chapter (such as abuse of power, allegations of corruption and the need to develop more effective mechanisms of accountability), but also involves allegations of racism (discussed in Chapters 3 and 7) and the methods of policing (referred to in Chapter 2).

Exam Hints

Answering short questions about police governance

1 Outline one way in which policing has become more centralised since 1979.

This question requires a discussion of any one way in which policing has departed from its historic localised character since 1945. There are a range of areas which could be discussed, including changes to the governance of policing (such as the desire of the 1979–97 Conservative government to exercise enhanced control over the service), or changes to the structure and organisation of policing, brought about by factors such as the policing of public disorder or the changing nature of crime (including its international characteristics). Whatever the example used, you should also discuss how such a change has been brought about, and the problems associated with such a development.

Answering essay questions about police governance

2 What changes have occurred to police powers since 1979?

This question involves two key areas. The first is the way in which police powers have increased since 1979, and an appreciation of why such a development has occurred. Here you could cite reasons which include the growth and political importance of crime as a political issue (discussed in Chapter 2), and the increase in public disorder (the topic of Chapter 3).

The second is concerned with the manner in which police powers have been subject to regulation (especially the safeguards regarding the use of certain powers contained in the 1984 Police and Criminal Evidence Act). The importance of police powers to police-public relationships could also be discussed in connection with events described above, and in connection with styles of policing referred to in Chapter 2, and allegations of racism discussed in Chapters 3 and 7.

Practice Questions

1 Discuss any one reform which the 1979-1997 Conservative governments made to policing in England and Wales.

2 Why have police actions been the subject of public debate since 1979?

7

RACIALLY-MOTIVATED VIOLENCE

Introduction

THIS CHAPTER LOOKS at racially-motivated violence in the UK. Particular attention is devoted to the police service, examining the way in which police actions have infringed the civil liberties of ethnic minority communities, and evaluating the adequacy of their response to racially-motivated violence.

Key points
This chapter will discuss the following key issues:

- reforms introduced into the police service after 1981 to combat racism, which led to violations of the civil liberties of ethnic minorities
- the adequacy of the response by the police service to racial violence
- the impact of the Macpherson report into the botched murder investigation of Stephen Lawrence on the police service, and the subsequent implementation of this report by the Labour government
- the need for further action by the State to combat racially-motivated violence.

THE POLICE SERVICE AND ETHNIC MINORITIES

This section examines the extent to which reforms introduced into the police service after the Scarman report in 1981, succeeded in eliminating racism which had previously infringed the civil liberties of ethnic minorities.

THE IMPACT OF REFORMS INSTITUTED AFTER 1981

Following the disorders in 1981, a series of reforms were put forward. This section briefly analyses the impact of key recommendations on the police service.

Recruitment

Changes in the racial make-up of Britain's police forces proved very difficult to achieve, in spite of pressure exerted by the House of Commons Home Affairs Committee and the Home Office. The expenditure of £1 million to attract ethnic minority recruits only increased their number to 467 (less than 2 per cent of the total number of officers) by 1990.

A number of reasons may explain this situation. The attempt to improve police–ethnic community relationships was based on the assumption that the recruitment of more black officers would achieve this goal. However, the negative image of the police within such communities meant that members of minorites who joined the police ran the risk of rejection by their peers, as well as the possibility of being subjected to racial prejudice from white officers who constituted the bulk of Britain's police personnel. Such factors also explained the high wastage rate of recruits from ethnic minority communities.

Training

Reforms to eradicate racist behaviour from police forces were introduced into training programmes in the wake of the Scarman report. However, these failed to achieve immediate dramatic improvements in police attitudes. There are a number of explanations for such failings. One problem concerned the philosophy underlying the approaches which were adopted. A considerable difference exists between multi-cultural and anti-racist training programmes. The former suggest that the problems which sometimes occur between races are based upon misunderstandings, which can be remedied by providing information on the history and background of minority communities. The latter, however, insists that racial intolerance will only be remedied when members of the dominant culture become aware of their own racism, and then become receptive to ways designed to remedy their own acknowledged defects. Police training was mainly of the multi-cultural variety and was perhaps insufficiently challenging to tackle racism in the police service.

THE REFORM OF POLICE CULTURE

Attempts to eradicate racism within police forces have been traditionally directed at the external issue of police–public relationships. An alternative approach is to concentrate on the internal characteristics of the police service, especially its culture, one core characteristic of which is alleged to be racial prejudice. Tackling those processes which cause and reproduce racism (particularly the marginalisation of black officers) within police forces, is an indispensable requirement for eliminating the public display of such behaviour towards members of ethnic minorities. Such an approach will ensure that reforms to police recruitment and training policies are advanced within an organisational climate which is supportive of initiatives to eradicate racism.

PROBLEMS AFFECTING POLICE-ETHNIC MINORITY RELATIONSHIPS IN THE 1990s

The perception that reforms recommended by Lord Scarman had failed to improve the relationship between police and ethnic minority communities was evidenced by a number of problems which surfaced during the 1990s. These problems suggested that the police service continued to contravene the civil liberties of ethnic minorities, by pursuing discriminatory practices towards them.

The continuance of urban disorder
Disorders linked to police relations with ethnic minority communities continued after 1981. In 1985 riots occurred in:

- *Handsworth, Birmingham*: these followed a number of confrontational situations between the police and young black people.
- *Brixton*: these occurred after the police shooting of Cherry Groce, which occurred when police raided her home looking for her son, in connection with a robbery (of which he was later acquitted).
- *Haringey's Broadwater Farm Estate*: these took place after the death of Cynthia Jarrett from a heart attack caused by a police raid on her house, in connection with enquries related to her son.

Although the profile of the areas involved in urban disorder altered in the 1990s, the relationship between the police and ethnic minority communities remained a factor in episodes such as the riots in Manningham, Bradford, in 1995.

Police tactics
By the late 1980s most police forces had established discrete units concerned with race and community relations, typically based at headquarters and divisional level. These, however, failed to permeate all aspects of policing, implying that race relations issues were matters of concern only to a small number of specialist officers. Additionally the tendency to utilise confrontational tactics to respond to threats (apparent or actual) posed to law enforcement in inner-city areas, resulted in the deterioration of police–public relationships in such areas.

The continued articulation and practice of racism
Senior officers have sometimes been associated with public comments which are perceived as racist, in particular alleging that black people perpetrate particular types of crime. This serves to establish a 'black–youth–crime linkage' in both the

eyes of the public and the police, who may subsequently find it difficult to appreciate black youths as victims of crime. This linkage of race and crime was made in 1995 when the Metropolitan Commissioner, Sir Paul Condon, stated that 80 per cent of muggings in high crime areas including Harlesden, Stoke Newington and Lambeth were carried out by young black men. This statement implied that the colour of a person's skin and not socio-economic factors such as poverty and high unemployment were responsible for certain types of crime. It was contradicted by the *Independent* on 8 July 1995, which asserted that, nationwide, 80 per cent of persons in prison for this type of offence were white.

Other police practices were alleged to have discriminated against ethnic minorities. These included the following:

Cautioning policy

Arrested black people are less likely to be cautioned and more likely to be sent to prison. This helps to account for 18 per cent of the prison population being non-white.

Use of force

In 1993, Joy Gardner choked on her own vomit while restrained in a body-belt. An Old Bailey Jury cleared two police officers of manslaughter in 1995. A third officer was cleared on the directions of the judge earlier in the trial. The Police Complaints Authority did not subsequently insist that these three officers should face disciplinary charges. The acquittal of these police officers led Bernie Grant MP to articulate the outrage of many black people when he stated that the tendency for the deaths of black people in custody to go unpunished suggested that 'a black life is worth nothing'. In 1999, a report by the Police Complaints Authority warned the police against handcuffing detainees behind their backs while they were lying on the ground, in order to prevent positional asphyxia which had led to the deaths of several black people who had died in police custody in the previous three years. The report emphasised, however, that the 147 persons who had died in police custody in this period included only 12 black people.

Corruption

Allegations that drugs had been planted on young black persons at Stoke Newington police station (in Hackney, London), were made in the 1990s. These were the subject of an investigation which gave rise to 31 civil actions against the police. In one of these, a black minicab driver was given an out-of-court settlement of £70,000.

Stop and search and arrest

The issue of stop and search and arrest has an important bearing on the relationship between the police and ethnic minorities. If these police powers are disproportionately used against black people, it would support allegations that the police deliberately target members of such communities, perceiving them to be a disruptive element in society which needs to be controlled. The amended stop and search provisions of the 1994 Criminal Justice and Public Order Act (which removed the condition of reasonableness that a prohibited article would be found) may serve to intensify perceptions of racism, unless they are effectively monitored in accordance with the safeguards contained in the 1984 Police and Criminal Evidence Act and the 1991 Criminal Justice Act.

STOP, SEARCH AND ARREST

> The accusation of bias in the police use of stop and search powers remain. In 1997/8, one million stop and searches were carried out under the Police and Criminal Evidence Act, of which 11 per cent were of black people and 5 per cent Asian, both groups accounting for 166,000 stops and searches. In 1999, a report by the organisation, Statewatch, stated that black people were 7.5 times more likely to be stopped and searched, and four times more likely to be arrested than white people, and that in 15 of the 43 police forces in England and Wales, one in five of the black population aged over 10 had been arrested in the past year. Merseyside police had one of the highest rates, with nearly one in three black people aged over 10 arrested.

THE POLICE SERVICE AND RACIALLY-MOTIVATED VIOLENCE

The previous section has argued that reforms introduced into the police service after 1981 failed to prevent continued police infringements of the civil liberties of ethnic minorities. The following discussion asserts that police inertia in connection with racially-motivated violence further aggravated this situation, and indicated a basic failure in the State's commitment to human rights.

CIVIL LIBERTIES AND HUMAN RIGHTS

Civil liberties are primarily concerned with the relationship between the government and the governed of a specific country. They include many basic 'freedoms' including that of speech and assembly.

Human rights consist of basic entitlements such as the right to 'life, liberty and the pursuit of happiness' which ought to be accorded to all human beings. Such are therefore universal in application. Human rights are frequently expressed in terms of ideals (such as equality of treatment) which may be given substance by specific enactments. An important statement of these is found in the 1948 United Nations Universal Declaration of Human Rights.

Racial violence must be viewed in the context of the denial of human rights to those who are victims of it. It is based upon a rejection of the shared humanity of people of all races, it undermines their liberty and security, and seeks to perpetuate an unequal power relationship between white and black people. An effective human rights policy must therefore give pre-eminent attention to the eradication of violence of this nature.

THE EXTENT OF RACIAL VIOLENCE

Since 1979, members of ethnic minority communities have frequently been subject to various forms of racially-motivated violence, ranging from verbal abuse and incivility, to physical attacks on themselves and their property. In 1998 a Home Office report stated that the total of racist incidents in 1997–8 was 13,880. Official figures, however, are believed to provide an inaccurate picture of the problem, as racial attacks are frequently not reported: the 1996 British Crime Survey reported that there were 140,000 racially-motivated incidents. These attacks are inflicted upon individuals or groups purely because of their colour, race, nationality or ethnic and national origins. Racial harassment may be targeted at individuals who become subject to a sustained campaign of intimidation, or it may be randomly directed at individuals. In 1994 the House of Commons Home Affairs Committee declared that racial violence constituted a most serious threat to social harmony: 'an assault motivated by racism is more socially-divisive than any other assault, and if allowed to pass unchecked will begin to corrode the fabric of our tolerant society'.

Accusations of police ineffectiveness in responding to racially-motivated violence were made in the 1990s. Perceived indifference to such episodes indicated that people on the receiving end were officially regarded as second class citizens who, in contravention of the rule of law, were denied protection by the law, while the perpetrators of such violence were seemingly above it.

THE STEPHEN LAWRENCE MURDER AND THE MACPHERSON REPORT

The failure of the police service to deal adequately with racial violence was highlighted by the response of the Metropolitan police to the murder of a black teenager, Stephen Lawrence, on April 22, 1993. This murder proved to be a major catalyst emphasising the need for change in the way in which police forces, and especially the Metropolitan police, responded to racial violence.

RACIST MURDERS

Racist murders were a major problem in the 1990s.

- On 24 February 1999, the *Guardian* published a list of 25 black and Asian people (in addition to Stephen Lawrence) who had been murdered in racially-motivated attacks since 1991.
- A Home Office report in 1998 reported that murderers of black people were less likely to be caught than those of white or other ethnic groups.
- In 1998 the organisation Statewatch reported that suspects were identified in 90 per cent of cases where white people had been murdered. The figure for the murders of black people was 60 per cent.
- It was alleged that the police were often disinclined to view any racial motive in such murders and, in connection with the death of the musician Michael Menson, they failed for 18 months, to perceive the incident as murder at all, alternatively viewing the attack as a self-inflicted injury.

There were two damning criticisms of the manner in which the subsequent investigation was handled – the failure by officers at the scene of the crime to assess any racial factor in the murder, and the delay occasioned in arresting suspects. The first arrests occurred on 7 May, although (as the Macpherson report stated) important information on this matter had been received by the investigating team soon after the murder had taken place. Two persons were subsequently charged with murder, but the CPS dropped the charges on 29 July on the grounds of insufficient evidence. In 1994 the CPS again declined to prosecute. The Lawrence family subsequently initiated a private prosecution against three youths allegedly involved in the attack, but this broke down in 1996 when the trial judge ruled that the identification of two of the defendants by Duwayne Brooks (who had been attacked with Lawrence) was contradictory and contaminated.

In 1998, the Labour government initiated an inquiry into this issue which was chaired by a retired judge, Sir William Macpherson. In 1999, his report was fiercely critical of the police handling of this matter. He examined three specific allegations in connection with it – that the Metropolitan police were:

- incompetent
- racist
- corrupt.

Macpherson found the Metropolitan police guilty of the first two accusations, cold comfort being drawn from the fact that he did not endorse the charge of corruption. Sir William stated that the investigation had been fundamentally flawed and 'marred by a combination of professional incompetence, institutional racism, and a failure of leadership by senior officers'. He stated that the police were guilty of 'gross negligence' in their investigation of this murder, an accusation which hinged on the failure of the police to make early arrests.

In 1981, Lord Scarman's report largely attributed racism in the police service to attitudes held by a small minority of officers. Macpherson, however, went further than this, effectively arguing that racism existed throughout the Metropolitan police. He advanced the concept of institutional racism which his report defined as 'the collective failure of an organisation to provide an appropriate and professional service to people because of their colour, culture or ethnic origin. It can be seen or detected in processes, attitudes and behaviour which amount to discrimination through unwitting prejudice, ignorance, thoughtlessness and racist stereotyping which disadvantage minority ethnic people'.

Macpherson's report suggested a number of reforms (70 in total). These included:

Rebuilding the confidence of the ethnic minority communities in policing

Macpherson's first recommendation was that a ministerial priority should be established to increase the trust and confidence in policing amongst minority ethic communities. It was proposed that performance indicators should be used to monitor its implementation, such as the existence of strategies for recording, investigating and prosecuting of racist incidents, measures to encourage such incidents to be reported and the extent of multi-agency cooperation and information exchange. A major problem with attaining this objective concerned the image of the police. In 1999 a *Guardian*/ICM poll showed that one in four members of the general public believed that the police were racist. Thirty-three per cent of respondents believed that the police failed to treat black or Asian people fairly, and only 45 per cent disagreed with this proposition.

Definition of racist incidents
The police service had traditionally been unwilling to accept the racial motivation for racist crimes. Macpherson sought to solve this problem by providing a definition of racist incidents. These should be defined as 'any incident which is perceived to be racist by the victim or any other person', and the term should be understood to include both crimes and non-crimes in policing terms. Both should be recorded and investigated with equal commitment.

The recruitment of more black and Asian police officers
This recommendation of Macpherson echoed that of Scarman in 1981. In 1998 the ethnic minority population comprised 5.6 per cent of the total population. However, there were only 2,483 black or Asian police officers in all English and Welsh police forces (which constituted 2 per cent of the total personnel of 124,885). This was a particular problem in London where the ethnic minority community comprised 19.2 per cent of the population but only 3.3 per cent of the Metropolitan police's 28,000 officers were drawn from such communities. In 1999:

- there were 873 ethnic minority officers in the Metropolitan police
- eight police forces had seven or fewer black or Asian officers
- a report by the Inspectorate asserted that only three forces in England and Wales (the Metropolitan police, West Yorkshire and South Wales) were making sufficient efffort to recruit and retain officers from ethnic minority backgrounds.

To consider whether the use of racist language and behaviour and the possession of offensive weapons in a private place should become a criminal offence
This suggestion was prompted by evidence obtained from a police surveillance video, which showed some of those accused of Stephen Lawrence's murder acting in a violent manner and using vicious, racist language. A 'private place' would include the home, but extend to other venues such as clubs and meeting places.

Freedom of information legislation should extend to most areas of policing
This proposal was designed to make allegations of incompetence and prejudice easier to prove in the future, and went further than the recommendation in the

1998 White Paper on this subject, which included documents relating to the administrative functions of the police but excluded material related to the investigation and prosecution functions of the police.

Reform of the 1976 Race Relations Act

This reform would bring to entire public sector within the scope of the legislation, thus enabling the Commission for Racial Equality (CRE) to launch investigations into individual police forces. It would leave officers facing claims for damages of discrimination from those they had mistreated.

To consider the abolition of double jeopardy

This would enable the Court of Appeal to permit a person to be re-tried, having initially been acquitted, if fresh and viable evidence subsequently became available. It was put forward as a solution to the acquittal of three defendants in the Lawrences' private prosecution in 1996.

The introduction of a tougher police disciplinary regime

It was proposed that racist words or actions should lead to disciplinary proceedings, which would normally result in an officer's dismissal from the service. It was also proposed that disciplinary action should be available for at least five years after an officer had retired. This suggestion was especially influenced by the fact that a number of senior officers whose conduct with regard to the Lawrence investigation had been criticised by the PCA, had retired from the police service and were thus unable to face neglect of duty charges.

THE IMPLEMENTATION OF THE MACPHERSON REPORT

In March 1999, the Metropolitan police published a report, *A Police Service for All the People*. This was compiled by a working party from the public and private sectors, including the CRE. It put forward a 15-point plan designed to tackle institutional racism. One objective was to have a fifth of senior posts held by ethnic minority officers, to be achieved by introducing a special career development scheme for officers of the rank of inspector and above. In 1999, only four ethnic minority officers in this force were of superintendent rank.

The issue of recruitment was addressed through suggestions that fellowships could be made available to ethnic minority students in their final year of study, to encourage them to join the police service following graduation. Retention of such officers was proposed to be tackled by establishing network groups of 30–35 ethnic minority officers across London, each with career development officers attached to them. Mentoring schemes would also be introduced to aid isolated ethnic minority offficers.

The government's response to the Macpherson report

The Home Secretary, Jack Straw was keen to ensure that the existence of racism in society would not be used as an excuse for the racist behaviour of individual officers. He indicated that all members of the police service should address this problem, with senior officers having an important role in challenging racist behaviour and language by their staff. In March 1999, he announced the government's response to the proposals of the Macpherson report which were contained in an 'action plan'. This included:

- *definition of racist incidents*: Macpherson's definition of a racist incident was accepted, although this would only be used in the initial reporting of an incident, and would not determine the issue of racial motivation when someone was charged and placed on trial
- *race relations legislation*: the proposal to extend the legislation to cover the whole of the public sector, including the police service, was accepted
- *freedom of information legislation*: all aspects of policing, including operations, would be subject to such legislation when it was introduced, although information relating to investigations and informers would be exempt
- *racism awareness training*: all officers (including the CID) would be trained in racism awareness and how to value cultural diversity
- *police discipline*: new regulations came into effect in April 1999 which meant that racist behaviour in any officers would result in their dismissal. The proposal that disciplinary action should be available for five years after an officer retired would be reviewed by the Home Secretary, who would also consider legislation to enable forfeiture of police pensions for serious disciplinary offences
- *stop and search*: the Home Secretary would consider whether a written record with reasons for all stops should be given to those searched
- *an independent complaints system*: the government was sympathetic to an independent system for investigating complaints against the police, and a feasibility study would consider the costs of such a system.

The issue of reforming double jeopardy was referred to the Law Commission, and reservations were expressed concerning the practicability of banning racist language and possessing offensive weapons in private places. It was also announced that the Metropolitan police would be subject to a review (conducted by the Inspectorate) of 25 racist murder cases where no one had been brought to justice. A steering group, chaired by the Home Secretary and which first met in May 1999, was set up to oversee the implementation of most of Macpherson's recommendations. The group would include the CRE and the Black Police Association.

Recruitment, retention and promotion
The Home Secretary had formerly endorsed proposals for a national target of 7 per cent for black and Asian officers, and he committed himself to imposing targets governing recruitment, promotion and retention of black and Asian officers at a speech delivered to the Black Police Association in October 1998. In a

subsequent speech to a conference of chief constables in April 1999, he announced Home Office targets for recruiting black and Asian officers for every force, in proportion to the ethnic mix of their local population, which were to be achieved over the next ten years. This would involve the Metropolitan police recruiting 5,662 minority officers to reflect the ethnic make-up of London's population. Areas with low black and Asian populations (such as Devon, Cornwall or Dorset) were set a 1 per cent baseline for ethnic recruitment. He further drew attention to the need to tackle the retention and promotion of officers from ethnic minority backgrounds. One difficulty immediately identified with this approach was financial constraints. Many police forces (including West Yorkshire which policed multi-ethnic Bradford) were having to scale down recruitment because of financial constraints.

'The Democratic Piece of the Jigsaw'

A further reform might be to subject the police to enhanced accountability. On 24 February 1999, Jonathan Freedland, writing in the *Guardian*, suggested that the Stephen Lawrence investigation could not have been handled so incompetently had the Commissioner of Police been accountable to the voters of London with its large ethnic electorate. He further suggested that if, alternatively, the Commissioner was accountable to a mayor (as is the case in New York), this episode would not have arisen either, since the mayor would have sacked the police chief in order to keep his/her own job. Although London will elect its first mayor in 2000, this official will not appoint the Commissioner of police, and neither is the Commissioner elected by the London voters. The enhanced role of local government in police affairs provided for by the 1998 Crime And Disorder Act does, however, open the possibility for increased indirect accountability of the police to their local public.

RACISM AND OTHER AGENCIES IN THE CRIMINAL JUSTICE SYSTEM

Accusations of police indifference to racially-motivated violence are important, since they act as the gateway to the legal system whereby those people guilty of such offences can be punished.This section briefly assesses the manner in which other agencies in the criminal justice system have responded to racially motivated violence.

RACIAL VIOLENCE AND THE JUDICIAL SYSTEM

The Crown Prosecution Service

Perceptions that the CPS had a poor record in dealing with racist violence led the Home Affairs Committee in 1989 to recommend the introduction of a comprehensive scheme of monitoring racial incident cases. This system would include the proportion of cases discontinued or downgraded by the CPS, and the reasons for such actions. However, such advice was not immediately acted upon. In 1992 the Code for Crown Prosecutors was amended so that a clear racial motive would be regarded as an aggravating feature when assessing whether a prosecution was required in the public interest.

The following year, the CPS began to monitor racial incident cases, and in 1995 set up the Racial Incident Monitoring Scheme to track racial crime. One benefit of this approach is that the CPS were more easily able to discern a racial motivation to a crime, even if the police had failed to identify this as an element. The file is then sent back to the police with the request that a racial incident report form should be included.

In 1999 the Macpherson report recommended that the police service and CPS should ensure that care was taken at all stages of a prosecution to recognise and include reference to any evidence of racial motivation. In particular it should be the duty of the CPS to ensure that such evidence was referred to, both at the trial and in the sentencing process. Additionally the CPS and Counsel should ensure that such evidence should not be excluded as the consequence of 'plea bargaining'. It was also proposed that the CPS should ensure that all decisions to discontinue a prosecution should be carefully and fully recorded in writing.

The Courts

Accusations of inappropriate treatment by the courts have been made in connection with racially-motivated violence, which gives rise to a perception that a black life is worth less than that of a white. One problem has been the reluctance of some judges to attach sufficient importance to the racial motivation of violent behaviour. For example:

- *1993*: two youths subjected an Asian teenager to an attack which left him partly blinded in one eye, but were jailed for only three and a half years. According to the *Independent* on 22 September 1993, the trial judge admitted that 'we are going to kill you, you smelly Paki' constituted racial undertones but did not amount to an 'aggravating feature'.
- *1998*: a judge imposed a sentence of two years probation and 100 hours community service on two white youths who launched an unprovoked attack on a black teenager, breaking his nose and calling him a 'stinking nigger'. The judge expressed satisfaction that there was 'no deep-seated racist attitude or hatred'.

The attitude of the courts in dealing with cases related to racial violence is not, however, totally biased. There are examples of those found guilty of racial attacks being given severe sentences. In 1997–8, a report by the CPS indicated that there were 1506 defendant cases in England and Wales, an increase of 161 on the previous year. Eighty-three per cent of those prosecuted in 1997–8 were convicted.

Legislative reform
The 1998 Crime and Disorder Act introduced a range of provisions to deal with racially-aggravated offences. It is perceived that the stiffer sentences provided for racially-motivated crime under this legislation, will have a significant effect on how offenders are prosecuted and sentenced. Even if a person is not charged with an offence under this legislation, the court is required to impose an increased penalty if it is satisfied that the offence met the new statutory requirements.

LIMITS TO POLITICAL TOLERATION

Political toleration is based on the view that individuals should be free to hold whatever views they wish. However, there are limits to toleration in any society, which arise when the articulation of such views gives rise to sentiments or actions which are harmful to other citizens. In such cases, the State may rightfully intervene to protect those who are subject to verbal or physical attack.

Such intervention could take the form of banning racist parties or organisations which directly or indirectly promote racial violence. This could be achieved by the extending the provisions of anti-terrorist legislation to those groups which use violence for political ends. This reform would have a useful effect of ensuring that the police service and judiciary were made fully aware of Parliament's intention to curb such activities.

The initiation of a campaign of planting nail bombs in April 1999 in Brixton (which injured 39 people) and in the East End of London (which injured five people) provided a justification for this legislative action. Although responsibility for these outrages was claimed by far-right organisations, the police subsequently arrested a person with no links to groups such as Combat 18, or a splinter group, the White Wolves. These events, however, legitimate Macpherson's suggestion regarding the articulation of racism in a private place.

The random and indiscriminate nature of these attacks (whose display of opposition to multi-culturalism was subsequently extended to Britain's gay community) illustrates most clearly that racial violence cannot be viewed merely as a problem experienced by those individuals subjected to such actions, since it challenges the right of all ethnic minorities to live in Britain.

Aftermath of the Brick Lane bombing, 24 April 1999

SUMMARY

After reading this chapter you should be able to evaluate:

- the reasons why the Scarman report (1981) failed to have a significant impact on subsequent police practices, which continued to violate the civil liberties of ethnic minorities
- the nature and extent of racially-motivated violence
- the rationale for the recommendations put forward in Sir William Macpherson's report into the handling by the Metropolitan police of the murder investigation of Stephen Lawrence, and the progress made in implementing these reforms
- the extent to which further measures are required to combat racially-motivated violence, and the reasons why adequate responses to racially-motivated violence form an essential aspect of an effective human rights policy.

STUDY 🅿 GUIDES

Revision Hints

Inadequate State responses to racial violence may form a specific field of study, but can also be linked to the issue of race relations in Britain, especially the failure to counter racism in society. You can present material which is concerned with enhanced measures being taken by the State to curb racist violence, within the context of the extent to which liberal democratic systems of government should place curbs on civil liberties and political activities. Questions may also be asked concerning the relationship between the police and ethnic minority communities. This could also be linked to a discussion of police styles and methods contained in Chapters 2, 3 and 6 in addition to this chapter.

Exam Hints

Answering short questions on the State's response to racial violence

1   Give one argument in favour of banning racist parties or organisations and one argument against.

This question regarding political toleration requires you to present a case for banning a party or organisation advocating racist politics. You might argue that such bodies legitimise targeted and randomly-directed violence against ethnic minorities, or that banning focuses the minds of the police and judiciary on the need to combat racism in contemporary society. The case against could include a consideration of issues such as maytrydom or the way in which this reform might drive parties underground and make it more difficult for the state to monitor them. Strengthen the assessment by considering how racism is expressed (words or violent deeds), and the extent to which a liberal democratic state should place limits on political activities.

Answering essay questions on racial violence

2   What effect did the murder of Stephen Lawrence in 1993 have on the State's response to combat racism?

This question requires a discussion of the inadequate way in which the State in general and the Metropolitan police in particular responded to this murder. You should address specific criticisms of this response, including the failure of the police to offer an acceptable level of service to ethnic minority communities, and an assessment of why this was the case. You should also be familiar with the main recommendations of the Macpherson report (1999) on the police, and the way in which the Labour government responded to these suggestions. Suggest what further measures could be taken to curb racially motivated violence (such as the banning or racist parties and/or organisations such as Combat 18).

Practice Questions

1 With reference to events which have taken place since 1979, analyse the evidence for suggesting that actions taken by the police service contravened the civil liberties of members of ethnic minority communities.

2 Outline any *one* recommendation contained in the Macpherson report (1999) into the murder of Stephen Lawrence and discuss the subsequent progress made in implementing it.

CONCLUSION

The study of crime, disorder, the judiciary and police service is important for students of politics for three reasons.

First, crime and disorder are key issues in contemporary politics. We need to understand why these issues emerge, and the way in which the political parties seek to address them. We should be particularly aware of the causes and responses to various manifesations of extra-parliamentary political activities, at which disorder sometimes occurs.

Second, although the judiciary and police service have historically claimed a wide degree of independence from 'outside' control, they operate within a political environment. The mechanisms of accountability of the agencies which operate within the criminal justice system are important. As students of politics, we need to be able to evaluate the nature of these arrangements, the changes which governments introduce, and the impact of these changes.

Finally, civil liberties are key concerns in a liberal democratic political system. We need to understand the way these rights are protected by the state and the judicial system and the nature of reforms to secure them more adequately. In particular, students of politics need to appreciate the nature of racially-motivated violence, and understand why a vigorous response to this problem is a cardinal principle of an effective human rights policy. The response of the State to racial violence should be viewed within the context of limits to political toleration.

The material contained in this book should be supplemented by your own, wider study. Some suggestions for further reading of published material are made at the end of this book. However, when preparing for examinations it is important to be as up-to-date in your material as possible. In particular you should be able to provide contemporary examples to illustrate your arguments. These can be most readily obtained by regularly reading a quality newspaper, and will help to emphasise the importance of the topics covered in this book to the study of contemporary political affairs.

GLOSSARY

Association of Chief Police Officers (ACPO) The senior ranks of the police service. It is consulted by the Home Office on a range of issues affecting law, order and police affairs and can also serve as a power interest group in these matters.

Civil liberties These provide citizens with rights which are legally enforceable, to protect them against actions undertaken by the government. Important civil liberties include the freedom from arbitrary arrest, freedom of speech, association, movement and assembly, and the right to a fair trial.

Clear up rates These are statistics which suggest the extent to which crime reported to the police has been solved. However, a crime can be regarded as 'cleared up' if a range of criteria other than the successful prosecution of an offender are fulfilled.

Core and ancillary functions of the police This is concerned with defining the key responsibilities of police forces – differentiated from other functions performed by the police, could be carried out by other agencies, perhaps in the commercial sector. The attempt to define core functions was investigated by a team chaired by Ingrid Posen in 1993 .

Criminal Cases Review Commission (CCRC) This was established in 1997 and took over the Home Office's responsiblity for examining alleged miscarriages of justice.

Crown Prosecution Service (CPS) The operations of this body are governed by the 1985 Prosecution of Offences Act. It assumed responsibility for prosecutions formerly conducted by the police.

Diplock Courts This was a system of trial before a judge without the use of a jury. It was introduced into Northern Ireland in 1973 in connection with 'scheduled offences' (ie, crimes concerned with politically motivated violence).

Europol This development (which is in its infancy) is concerned with police organisation operating across national boundaries in the EU. It is compatible with a range of other political reforms to achieve a single European state.

Extra-parliamentary political activity Political activities which are undertaken outside of Parliament and are designed to influence political decisions. Methods such as demonstrations, industrial disputes and riots are examples.

Human rights These embrace many of the civil liberties referred to above. These are put forward, however, as core values which should exist universally, rather than be provided for on a country-by-country basis. This means, therefore, that human rights go beyond civil liberties by putting forward moral values which should exist in all nations.

Judicial review This process involves the judiciary scrutinising the actions taken by the legislature, executive or other tiers of government. One aspect of this process is to ensure that actions taken by the executive are strictly in accordance with the law.

Law Lords These are the most senior judges in Britain, who serve on the Appellate and Appeals Committee of the House of Lords, and also on the Judicial Committee of the Privy Council. They are appointed by the Queen on the recommendation of the Prime Minister.

Lord Chancellor This official is head of the judiciary but also serves in the other two branches of government, by virtue of being a member of the Cabinet and the House of Lords.

MI5 This agency (whose full title is the Security Service) was set up in the early years of the twentieth century to foil the spying activities of foreign countries in Britain. It was placed on a statutory basis by the 1989 Security Service Act. In 1992 it was given the lead role in combating terrorism on mainland Britain, and the 1996 Security Services Act also gave it the responsiblity for dealing with serious crime.

Multi-agency approach to crime prevention This suggests that the police alone cannot prevent crime, but require their activities to be coordinated with a range of other public sector bodies. The 1998 Crime and Disorder Act established formal machinery to secure this approach in connection with juvenile offending (in the form of Youth Offender Teams) and local crime prevention measures (Partnerships).

Mutual Aid A system whereby one police force can request aid from another, usually in connection of with a major public order incident. The system of mutual aid is governed by the 1964 Police Act.

National Crime Squad (NCS) Established by the 1997 Police Act, it is linked to investigating crime which is the concern of more than one police force in England and Wales.

National Criminal Intelligence Service (NCIS) Established in 1992, it brought together in one organisation a number of existing police intelligence-gathering units which operated on a national basis. It was controlled by the Home Office and placed on a statutory footing by the 1997 Police Act.

National Reporting Centre (NRC) This was established by ACPO in 1972. Its main role is to coordinate mutual aid in major public order incidents such as the 1984–5 miners' dispute, effectively enabling it to control the movement of police officers throughout the country. It was re-named the Mutual Aid Coordinating Centre following the miners' dispute.

Official crime statistics These figures seek to suggest the level of crime in society. They are based on incidents which are reported to the police and subsequently recorded by them.

Paramilitary policing A more coercive form of policing, based on the use of aggressive tactics and weaponry. It indicates a move away from the notion of minimum force.

Policing by objectives A system designed to secure enhanced value for money in the police service. Each force would prepare a mission statement to indicate its overall objectives. Action plans would then be devised to implement these objectives, and progress in attaining them would be monitored.

Rule of law This principle asserts the supremacy of the law as an instrument which governs the actions of individual citizens in their relations to each other, and also specifies the conduct of the State towards them. Requirements such as equality before the law, and basing punishment on formalised legal procedures, are important aspects of the rule of law.

Self report studies A method used to assess the level of crime in society, by asking respondents to a survey to indicate their personal involvement in carrying out such activities

Separation of powers This concept suggests that tyranny is avoided if the three branches of government (the legislature, executive and judiciary) are independent of each other. Although complete autonomy is impractical, in most liberal democracies the judiciary enjoys a relative degree of insulation from control exerted by the other two branches.

Service functions of the police Functions commonly carried out by the police but which are not linked to their role of law enforcement. Examples include visiting schools to advise children on road safety.

Social causes of crime Factors such as unemployment, poverty or deprivation, which are often regarded as circumstances underlying criminal behaviour. This view suggests that crime can thus be prevented by improving social conditions, rather than through measures which include tougher penalties to deter criminal activity.

Soundings A procedure in the appointment of judges. It involves the Lord Chancellor's Department seeking out the views of serving members of the judiciary on the suitability of a candidate for judicial office.

Strong State This argument asserts that measures such as the 1986 Public Order Act and the 1994 Criminal Justice and Public Order Act sought to curtail civil and political liberties, to enable the State to deal with the inevitable protests from those who suffered as the result of the introduction of the free market economy after 1979. This approach was viewed as the inevitable consequence of capitalism in crisis (the crisis being the decline in profits).

Three Strikes and You're Out! The popular term used in connection with the provisions of the 1997 Crime (Sentences) Act; a person with two previous convictions for domestic burglary would automatically receive a three-year prison sentence if convicted for a third time.

Tripartite system of police governance The division of responsibilities for policing between the Home Office, police authorities and chief constables. The system of checks and balances which governs the relationship between these three bodies.

Underclass A social group which is excluded from society by being denied privileges or opportunities available to other members of society.

Victimisation Studies A method of assessing the level of crime in society, by asking information from a cross-section of the population of their personal experience of the problem. This methodology is used by the British Crime Survey.

FURTHER READING

John Benyon and John Solomos, *The Roots of Urban Unrest*, (Oxford: Pergamon, 1987). Although now dated in terms of the events covered, this examination of urban disorder remains valid for the theoretical framework within which various explanations of such events are offered. See also John Benyon, Disadvantage, Politics and Disorder, (Leicester: Leicester University, 1993).

Paul Gordon, *White Law*, (London: Pluto Press, 1983). Although also dated, this provides a good account of racism in Britain. The central argument of the institutional racism of the criminal justice system remains highly relevant.

Richard Hodder-Williams, *Judges and Politics in the Contemporary Age*, (London: Bowerdean, 1996). This book analyses the political functions of the judiciary. It adopts a comparative approach, with much material derived from America and the UK. A more detailed account of the constitutional position of the British judiciary is to be found in Robert Stevens, *The Independence of the Judiciary*, (Oxford: Clarendon, 1997).

John Griffith, *The Politics of the Judiciary*, (London: Fontana, 1991, 4th edition). This book is *the* classic text on the political aspects of the role of the judiciary. The notion of corporate biases and prejudices, however, is challenged by other authors, including B. Roshier and H. Teff, *Law and Society in England*, (London: Tavistock Publications, 1980).

Frank Leishman, Barry Loveday and Stephen Savage (editors), *Core Issues in Policing*, (Harlow: Longman, 1996). This book provides an illuminating series of essays concerned with changes to the organisation and management of policing in Britain.

Diana Woodhouse, 'Politicians and the Judiciary: A Changing Relationship', *Parliamentary Affairs*, Volume 48, Number 3, July 1995, pages 401–417. A good discussion of the increased tendency of the judiciary to scrutinise the actions of the executive branch of government in the 1990s.

Michael Zander, *The Law-Making Process*, (London: Butterworths, 1994, 4th edition). This valuable account provides important information of the judiciary and its law-making role.

PRIMARY SOURCES

The Brixton Disorders 10-12 April 1981, Report of An Inquiry by the Rt Hon Lord Scarman, OBE, (London: HMSO, 1981, Cm 8427). This influential account of the causes of urban disorder initiated the reform of policing in the 1980s. However, Scarman was also aware of the importance of social conditions underpinning such behaviour.

Police Reform: The Government's Proposals for the Police Service in England and Wales, (London: HMSO, 1993, Cm 2281). This White Paper put forward the basis of the reform of the police service contained in the 1994 Police and Magistrates' Courts Act. It also provides a good critique of the operations of the tripartite system of police governance introduced in the 1964 Police Act.

The Bradford Commission Report: Report of an Inquiry into the Wider Implications of Public Disorders in Bradford, 9, 10 and 11 June 1995, (London: Stationery Office, 1996). This provides an important account of causes of urban disorder in the 1990s, with specific reference to events in Manningham.

House of Commons, Home Affairs Committee, Third Report, *Judicial Appointments Procedures,* (London: HMSO, 1996, House of Commons Paper 52–1). This provides a large volume of information concerning the current practices of judicial appointments and an analysis of reforms to this process.

Misspent Youth ... Young People and Crime, (Abingdon: Audit Commission Publications, 1996). This discussion of the shortcomings of the youth justice system helped promote reform which was embodied in the 1998 Crime and Disorder Act.

Reducing Offending: An Assessment of Research Evidence on Ways of Dealing with Offending Behaviour, (London: Home Office, 1998, Home Office Research Study 187). This work contains detailed evaluation of a range of methods (including policing strategies and sentencing policy) to prevent crime.

The Stephen Lawrence Inquiry: Report of an Enquiry by Sir William Macpherson of Cluny, (London: TSO, 1999). This is a fundamental report on the botched investigation by the Metropolitan police into the murder of Stephen Lawrence in 1993 which will set the agenda for the reform of policing into the twenty-first century.

INDEX